Praise for *Girl*

'Enlightening, relatable, warm and witty,
Girl is a must-read.' *Sunday Times Style*

'*Girl* is an essential, vital and urgent exploration
of Black womanhood that should be on everyone's
reading list. Every page is meaningful and a call for
empathy, hope and change. There is such power
in the stories that are told, from Kenya's own
experience – as a mother, as a journalist, as an
American in London, to Ebele Okobi's essay
on the unspeakable loss of a brother to police
brutality. If any book should enrich – and disrupt
– your life, let it be this.' *Harper's Bazaar* UK

'Powerful, intelligent and thought-provoking.
A must read for our times and beyond.' *ELLE* UK

'Kenya Hunt provocatively threads cultural
observations through relatable stories that
illuminate our current cultural moment
while transcending it.' *Refinery29*

'An essential book to help in becoming
an anti-racist ally.' *Dazed*

'A provocative, heart-breaking and frequently hilarious
collection of original essays on what it means to
be Black, a woman, a mother and a global citizen
in today's ever-changing world.' *Glamour* UK

'*Girl* speaks to the Black woman of today.'
Bethann Hardison, model and activist

GIRL

GIRL

Essays on Black womanhood

KENYA HUNT

ONE PLACE. MANY STORIES

HQ
An imprint of HarperCollins*Publishers* Ltd
1 London Bridge Street
London SE1 9GF

This edition 2020

1
First published in Great Britain by
HQ, an imprint of HarperCollins*Publishers* Ltd 2020

ISBN: 978-0-00-837197-5

MIX
Paper from
responsible sources
FSC
www.fsc.org   **FSC™ C007454**

Cover design by HQ 2020 with contribution from Matt McGuinness

Typeset by Type-it AS, Norway
Printed and bound in CPI Group, Croydon CR0 4YY

This book is produced from independently certified FSC™ paper
to ensure responsible forest management.

For more information visit: www.harpercollins.co.uk/green

For Breonna Taylor, Sandra Bland,
Atatiana Jefferson, Aiyana Stanley-Jones,
Tanisha Anderson, Oluwatoyin Salau,
Gynnya McMillen, Korryn Gaines, Riah
Milton, Joyce Curnell, Dominique Fells...

CONTENTS

INTRODUCTION

When I started this book, I was on maternity leave with my second son. The freedom of being home all day, every day, and the disorientation of an on-demand breastfeeding schedule oddly suited my writing. It meant that I was awake and journalling during those quiet moments in the night when everyone else was sleeping. I liked the solitude that came with being housebound for large chunks of time with a newborn. After years spent hopped up on adrenaline, it felt good to be off the work treadmill for a moment and to have an opportunity to reassess my life and recalibrate. Not to mention I appreciated having a break to just focus on my family and my writing, uninterrupted by morning commutes, extended work travel and deadlines.

But now, as I complete the book with this introduction more than a year later, I'm housebound for a different reason. We're more than four months into a global pandemic, as the novel coronavirus (COVID-19) steamrolls its way through the world, and eight weeks into a nationwide lockdown. The experience of working from home all day, while in a government-enforced quarantine, feels much less like a freedom, though it is most certainly a privilege.

Small acts we once took for granted like shaking a stranger's hand, hugging a friend, visiting loved ones or having dinner in a crowded restaurant, are not possible for the foreseeable. Now, we walk down the street wearing face masks, paranoid about who might have coughed just steps before. And we scrub and disinfect our groceries (purchased in a whirlwind of panic after waiting in socially distanced queues that stretch for blocks outside stores) with a rigour that just months ago would have been declared a symptom of obsessive compulsive disorder.

The basics — our health, the food on our tables, a walk outdoors, a deep inhale of fresh air — now feel like life's ultimate luxuries. But luxury's meaning changes with context and the pandemic has made the divisions that separate race and class painfully clear.

When the virus hit, a popular line began circulating that 2020 was the end of identity politics, that COVID-19 was the great equaliser that didn't see race or class. People of colour knew better. And the opposite turned out to be true as the news was confirmed. Black, Muslim, Latin and Asian communities were the hardest hit, and women (who make up the vast majority of 'essential workers') were shouldering the brunt of the load. The virus wasn't wiping the slate clean, it was deepening pre-existing inequalities.

I've watched close friends lose their loved ones, jobs and mental health to COVID-19. I've also watched dear friends, forced to reimagine their lives in the face of disruption, begin exciting new jobs, launch innovative new projects, and enter new romantic relationships. Throughout it all, I saw my friends and family more than we had in years, checking in on each other throughout the week on Zoom, FaceTime and Houseparty to make sure we were holding up okay in isolation as sickness, death and a crippled economy inched closer.

And just when it seemed like the news cycle and our collective angst couldn't get worse, we found joy, laughter and solidarity in the most unexpected places. At an enormous, spontaneous Instagram Live party put on by the American DJ D-Nice, I bumped into old friends I hadn't seen in years (old media colleagues, music industry mates and nightclubbing buddies) and the imaginary ones I had only ever followed from a distance (Michelle Obama, Janet Jackson, Rihanna and Tracee Ellis Ross to name a few).

Each one of our circumstances were uniquely different and yet we were all there, 100,000 of us united in isolation and our need for human connection. Weeks later, over 700,000 of us tuned in to a live stream music battle-turned-mutual appreciation session between two women responsible for soundtracking multiple generations of Black lives, Erykah Badu and Jill Scott, and then bonded for the next twenty-four hours over the endless stream of feel-good memes the evening produced. It was a night of sisterhood and healing. A celebration of *us*, and all our nuances. 'Most of the time, I'd prefer, I like to be a lady. Sometimes, I'm not. I'm a lot of things. Aren't we a lot of things?' Jill Scott said. We were all alone, together.

The show of numbers throughout these moments reminded us of our own agency and collective power, especially when the world erupted in protests over the videotaped murder of George Floyd, an unarmed Black man suffocated under the knee of a white police officer. We mobilised on both small local and sprawling global levels. We raised money for bail funds for protestors, called government officials and demanded arrests, and circulated petitions to defund the police. We protested, both in the streets and virtually. And we called out racism as and when we saw it. We said their names: George. Breonna. Ahmaud. Tony. Aiyana. Eric. Michael. Sandra. Tamir. Tony. Tanisha. Yvette. Rekia. Natasha. Kindra. Kimberlee. Joyce. Ralkina. Kayla. Gynnya. Korryn. And we did all of this in a matter of weeks, with black women powering much of the action, from organising marches and conducting justice work trainings to creating social media campaigns and assets that mobilised millions around a range of action plans. Throughout it all, we asserted our beauty and humanity in the face of tragedy, while continuing to go to work, mother our families and support our friends and relatives. We showed up, together.

So while the world looks radically different from how it did when I first began writing these essays, reflecting on a decade's worth of personal and cultural touchstones, the issues at its heart — belonging, connection, resilience and identity — remain. And as we re-evaluate our lives during one of the most pivotal years in modern history, and move forward towards a future that will be different from the one we imagined, I hope this book reminds you that even in the midst of chaos, we're here, loving, persevering, growing and finding the meaning in life as we go.

1 GIRL

Girl! GWORL. Gorl. Guhl. Gurl. Grrrrrlll.

'Mommy, why is it that every time you're on the phone or with your friends it's always girl, girl, girl, girl?' my son asked me two years ago, as I was tucking him into bed for the night. I was amused. Mostly at the sight and sound of myself through my five-year-old's eyes and ears — he had gotten my animated pacing and high-pitched intonation just right — but also at the idea that I used the word enough for him to pick up on it.

'I hadn't realised, sweets. Do I really say it that much?'

'Girl! You do,' he said with a childish smirk, before turning over and closing his eyes. I tried to swallow my laughter as I turned off the light and tiptoed out of the room.

In my life I've used many pet names for the people I know and love: sis, luv, beauty, lovebug, babes, hon, pumpkin, doodlebug, sweets, bae, dumpling and peanut among others. But throughout my evolving networks of friends — and especially so among my Black chosen sisters — one term of endearment remains: girl. Equal parts greeting, exclamation and rallying call all at once.

As long as I can remember, girl was the root word in the unique love language between Black women, regardless of age. 'Girl, you got it. Just go out there and do your best,' my mom, Precious, would say while giving me a pre-dance recital peptalk during my childhood in Virginia. 'Babygirl, you crazy,' my aunt, Gloria, all gregarious joy, would tell my little sister, April, scooping her up in a hug, upon discovering that the child had piled on her hair pieces, blouses and bangles in a game of dress-up.

'Hey, girl, hey,' my dorm-mate at university would say in a conspiratorial, hushed voice, unveiling a box of caffeinated soft drinks and Krispy Kreme donuts as we prepared to pull an all-nighter for one upcoming exam or another. 'Guuurl,' my friends and I would sing along to Destiny's Child's 'Girl' as we got dressed for a night out, placing extra emphasis on the vocal runs every time Beyoncé, Michelle and Kelly would hit the title word. 'Guuuuurl,' we would sing along, imploring our imaginary friend to let a philandering man go, adding a vocal run or two and a fluttering hand for extra dramatic effect. Girl was a one-word lingua franca that transcended class, generations and geography. A word we used with each other to show affection and acknowledge shared history, experiences and aspirations.

When I entered the working world as a graduate, I became conflicted about the colloquialism. On the one hand, I was steeped in feminist culture as an assistant editor at *Jane* magazine, an iconic title in the feminist publishing community. Girl was a polarising word.

Some viewed it as an infantilising condescension (that's 'womyn', please and thank you), others as an empowering subversion (hey riot grrrls).

And then there was the hipster racism I'd inevitably encounter at dive bars after work. Bearded white boys in flannel shirts telling me, 'You go girl', in an annoying mimicry of an equally annoying, old imitation of Black women that comedian Martin Lawrence popularised in his eponymous sitcom years before. Or young white gay men on the fashion party circuit who mistakenly thought their queerness excluded them from buying into cultural stereotypes, and who caused me to stiffen with their awkward greeting: 'Hey girl, I like your hair. Is it yours?'

I didn't recognise myself in any of the pantomimes, though this was clearly how many envisioned Black women — one neck-rolling monolith. I refused to play to type and fit in with a narrow idea of what Black women were supposed to be.

I felt more kinship with the plethora of girls in the Black and brown ballroom scene. Yes, the icons in *Paris Is Burning* popularised the now commonplace social media age lexicon that includes 'yassss', 'girl', 'read', and 'honey' to the mainstream. These expressions — essentially innocuous, everyday words given entirely new meanings — originated with us, Black women (cis and trans), and can be traced back through generations to our hair salons, kitchens and churches. So, I'd code switch, limiting the love language to conversations with my closest Black women friends and family members back home.

I hadn't quite realised the Americanness of this, though, until I moved to London from New York in late 2008 and felt the need to build up my own network of Black women friends after tiring of always being The Only in my work and social life. I befriended Ghanaian, Nigerian, Jamaican and Black British women with sharp opinions, bold voices and thriving careers. Women who didn't dot their anecdotes with a loud 'girl' for emphasis, or use it as an affectionate preface to a warm hug or effusive compliment. 'Girl, you did that.' So it dropped out of my daily lexicon, only coming out for marathon phone catch-ups with Stateside girlfriends.

But as a new wave of racial discourse and Black consciousness rolled in with the Obama administration in the late aughts, 'girl' took on a new life of its own, crossed the pond and worked its way through the entire diaspora. We became, in a word, magic.

Like most cultural touchpoints in the 2010s, it began with a Tweet. #BlackGirlsAreMagic was created by one CaShawn Thompson to counteract a wave of bad PR in the form of tired stereotypes and lies. No, of course we're not shrill, unmarriageable, ugly and uneducated. We are strong, beautiful, originators of movements and culture the world over. As I write this, I'm listening to the official #BlackGirlMagic playlist on Spotify, filled with music by women of colour from across the world: London, Los Angeles, Lagos, New York, Ekiti, Chicago and Atlanta, among others. There are Black Girl Magic T-shirts, books, book clubs and websites. Not that we needed the hashtag to tell us who we are — we don't need a hashtag as validation. But the shortened #Blackgirlmagic and the like, including #Blackgirljoy and #carefreeBlackgirl, took off, broadcasting to the world what we already knew: when it comes to excellence, we're not new to this (to quote Drake, vocal appreciator of Black women), we're true to this.

Some people are validation junkies, addicted to the likes and shares, the digital pats on the back. But I get my highs from the hit of underestimation. Give me a 'meh' and I'll make you eat it. Disregard me and I'll show you. I get a rise out of proving people wrong. During the many interviews I've given as a fashion editor about the lack of diversity in the business, people sometimes ask me, 'What does it feel like to make it in an industry filled with people who don't look like you?'

It's being 19 years old and told by a university professor in Charlottesville, Virginia to manage my expectations and try a career in teaching high school when I expressed a desire to move to New York and work in magazine publishing. It's being told to go back to the drawing board during a staff meeting at my second magazine publishing job in New York, when the editor dismissed my pitch about a story on teenage moms with the nonchalant and wholly inaccurate logic that it 'was no good because the story would just be about Black girls, and no one wants to read that.' It's an editor sitting next to you in the front row during New York Fashion Week and showing you a photo of the African tribeswoman who will be her toddler's nanny during an extended winter stay at a national reserve in South Africa. It's to be repeatedly asked to go on television to comment about why there are so few of you in media, television and fashion, as if it's the only subject you're qualified to speak about.

It's to be seated next to a model agency owner at a work dinner, who tells you you're pronouncing your name wrong. 'I know the most luxurious lodge in Keenya. Where do you like to stay when you're there? Surely you've been to the country before, no? Not even Nairobi? Then why did your parents name you Keenya? You pronounce it "Kehn-ya" you say? Not "Keenya"? Hmmmm, are you sure?' It's to restrain yourself from using the other kind of 'girl'—'Girl!' — as admonishment and verbal eye roll. The kind of 'girl' I use for women who test my patience, no matter what their race. As in, 'Girl, stop! Old white colonialists pronounce it this way.' It's to sit in a staff meeting and suggest a Black pop star for the cover only to be told, 'But we just had a Black woman on the cover last month. And it would be too weird to have two in a row.'

But that was then. And this is now, the age of Black Girl Magic in which we're owning the expansiveness of Blackness at its cross-section with womanhood, tracing its myriad shapes and textures, during a time when what it means to be a Black woman has permeated every level of public discourse from the unbelievably tragic (Sandra Bland, Breonna Taylor, Atatiana Jefferson, and a tragically long list of others) to the tragi-comical (Rachel Dolezal).

What and who is Black Girl Magic? She's Solange Knowles dressed in white, dancing on the streets of New Orleans. It's my favourite photo of Malia and Sasha Obama, with girlfriends, trailing behind their dad, as they deplane Air Force One. It's Black Lives Matter founders Patrisse Khan-Cullors, Alicia Garza and Opal Tometi galvanising a global movement against the brutalisation of Black bodies. And Bernardine Evaristo winning the Booker Prize, the first Black British author to do so. It's Chimamanda Ngozi Adichie interviewing Michelle Obama about her record-breaking book in front of a sold-out theatre in London. And a video clip of Michelle Obama congratulating Beyoncé on her record-breaking Netflix special, *Homecoming* — a rich, rousing, and very Black, tribute to historically Black universities. It's nineteen Black women being elected to judgeships in Texas, a longstanding conservative state, during the American midterm elections. And five Black women, their backgrounds spanning South Africa, Jamaica and America, winning the world's five most iconic beauty pageants, Miss America, Miss USA, Miss Teen USA, Miss World and Miss Universe. It's Black actresses, singers and models dominating UK and US women's magazines for the first time in history, in September 2018. And South African two-time Olympic 800m champion Caster Semenya declaring herself 'supernatural' as she sought to qualify for the Tokyo Olympics. It's Kamala Harris running for President. And all of us avowing our solidarity in the face of global pandemics and tragedy. Women, girls, daring to be true to the gradations of ourselves in a world where anyone not named Beyoncé, Rihanna or Lupita tends to get depicted as chronically angry, perennially overlooked, forever victimised, unfailingly ratchet, and more. That's not how I view myself. That's not how anyone I know views themselves.

The world expects the more familiar, stereotypical image of us as the server of side eyes and roller of necks. But Black Girl Magic is a celebration that frees us from the confines of narrow expectation or subtext.

Girl!

I began hearing the call-out beyond my network of Black girlfriends. 'Girl,' Kim Tatum said, greeting fellow trans activist Rhyannon Styles during a podcast episode I hosted during my time as an editor at British *ELLE*. We were discussing what it meant to be trans, an idea that had entered the mainstream for the first time through global headline makers such as *Orange Is the New Black* star Laverne Cox and writer Janet Mock.

'Damn, girl, you look fabulous,' an Instagram post by the body positivity activist BodyPosiPanda read, inviting women to embrace their most authentic, unfiltered selves and learn to love the back fat, stretch marks and acne scars.

'I've got your back, girl,' I overheard a middle aged white saleswoman say to her co-worker, hair streaked with grey, as she fixed a frozen cash register during a shopping trip.

In a way, the word had become a positive affirmation and a vocal show of unity in our age of outrage. Yet there is little written about its use in this way.

I've watched 'girl' come full circle, just as my relationship with it has. I now openly use it to show sisterly affection, shared cultural experiences or not — as do many Londoners I know. When I checked in on a pregnant friend in south London who had birthed a baby boy after three days of labour, her reply, a single word sent via text, spoke volumes about joy, exhaustion, relief and perseverance: 'Girl... '

She didn't need to say anything more.

At a women's festival at the Saatchi Gallery where I appeared as a speaker, the green room was a joyous din of loud laughter, chatty group hugs and enthusiastic 'hey girls' between authors, journalists, models, activists and athletes. On stage, I asked Halima Aden, the Kenyan-born woman who made history as the world's first hijabi supermodel, if she ever felt a weight of responsibility as A First. 'Well, girl, when you put it that way,' she laughed before admitting she does.

Here, 'girl' wasn't tied to any specific country of origin. Just as it wasn't during the London Women's March months later where protestors of all ethnicities and ages walked with placards featuring such ballsy messages as 'Girls just want to have fun-damental human rights' and 'Girls doing whatever the fuck they want.'

Girls! Girl. Gurl. Girl, hey. Girl, bye. Girl, stop. Girl, go. Girl, we see you, and feel seen.

2 NOTES ON WOKE

'Precisely at the point when you begin to develop a conscience you must find yourself at war with your society.'

— BALDWIN

Few things in the Internet age have not been named. And many things, even if they have been named, have been rechristened, and rebranded again and again.

Healthy food, sleep and exercise combined to become 'wellness' and 'clean living'. Down-time became 'self-care'. Role models were repackaged, simply, as 'Goals' (with a capital G). And goals (lower case 'g') in the traditional sense became 'intentions'. The practice of making those goals happen, meanwhile, is now called 'manifestation'.

On the more sober end of the spectrum 'racism' was sugar-coated to read 'unconscious bias' and 'white supremacy' became 'white nationalism'. On the Internet, no person, place or thing is exempt from rebranding. And in the process, the meaning evolves, twists and turns, and at times, gets lost. One of the biggest examples of this is the very old idea wrapped in thoroughly modern packaging called 'woke'.

As I write this, I'm staring at a fashion magazine with the coverline 'woke bespoke'. Next to it, a newspaper supplement featuring a dating diary on the search for 'Mr Woke'. On my desktop, a guide to a 'woke Christmas', and in the adjacent tab, an Internet rant in response to said guide demanding people and publishers leave all writing about wokeness to Black writers. In another tab, an article bemoaning the Great Awokening of American politics. Meanwhile, on British television, a debate rages between royal correspondents and pundits about whether the royal family's most polarising members, Meghan and Harry, have in fact become too woke for their own good.

But what is woke? Most online dictionaries define it as an awareness of inequality and other forms of injustice that are normally racial in nature — as in, Nelson Mandela or Malcolm X. A few describe the term as merely being 'with it' — as in every cool kid you knew at uni. And increasingly, these days, many use it as a pejorative term to describe someone who is a slave to identity politics. How can all three possibly be the same? It's a sensibility, a quality, a state of being, a feeling backed up by a set of actions, sometimes all those things at once.

I can't think of a word that reflects the era as well as 'woke' does. There's its relative newness (woke was born and grew up alongside social media), its popularity as a hashtag and its political implications and activist leanings. And then there are its many definitions — the word's nature changes with each rotation of the news cycle. There's also its journey crossing over from Black culture to the Internet and mainstream news. Appropriation! All qualities that are extremely particular to this moment in time.

Confession: I'm allergic to the word. (An affliction I first developed in 2016, when MTV declared the term the new 'on fleek'.) Ironic, considering I am textbook woke. I identify with what it was. But cringe at what it's become. And bristle at the way the word is now weaponised. The disparity compels me to interrogate the term and its evolution. As Susan Sontag said in *Notes on Camp*, which inspired this very study, 'no one who wholeheartedly shares in a given sensibility can analyse it; he can only, whatever his intention, exhibit it. To name a sensibility, to draw its contours and to recount its history, requires a deep sympathy modified by revulsion.' So let's consider what woke is, and what it isn't.

1. Woke extends to conversations around art, politics, economic and social class, gender inequality, trans rights and environmentalism. But woke in its original incarnation rests on activism and Blackness.

2. The essence of woke is awareness. What you are newly aware of (a pay gap, systemic racism, unchecked privilege, etc) and what to do with that newfound knowledge is the question. And the answer

keeps changing depending on who you talk to. But regardless, you've answered the wake-up call, pushed your way out of bed, and are now listening.

3. To be woke, in the original sense, is to understand James Baldwin's declaration that 'to be a Negro in this country and to be relatively conscious is to be in a rage almost all the time.' It's to understand the unique kind of exhaustion that comes from being perpetually attuned to discrimination. It's to be weary and wary. To be woke is to long for a day when one doesn't have to stay woke.

4. Woke blurs the lines between politics and pop culture. You can't have one without the other; the latter is how woke culture entered the public consciousness and is the thing that sustains its relevancy, for better and for worse.

5. Most date woke's origins back to the American singer songwriter Erykah Badu's anthemic political medley, 'Master Teacher' from her album *New Amerykah*, a work she released in 2008, two years after the birth of Twitter and eight months after Apple released a thing called the iPhone, two facts that are pertinent here because woke is a term that owes its popularity to both. Badu sings over a psychedelic collage of samples about a quest for what sounds like a new plane of enlightenment:

'I am known to stay awake
(A beautiful world I'm trying to find)'

She then imagines a world in which there are 'no

niggas, only master teachers' and reminds the listener, repeatedly, that she stays woke.

This is woke at its most pure: unapologetically Black and cryptic (only the woke recognise the woke). A word conceived by Black people for Black people. A word reminiscent of Spike Lee's famous cry to 'Wake uuuuuuuuup!' in his seminal film *School Daze*, as his character, a student at a fictitious historically Black university, demands his light-skin-worshipping, good-hair-seeking, sex-addicted peers wake up from self-hatred and materialism and become aware of the injustices in their community and, ideally, do something about it.

6.   You can find a pocket guide to the essence of woke in the chorus of Childish Gambino's single, 'Redbone', a Funkadelic-esque R&B song released in 2016 that warns, 'you better believe in something'. Equal parts lustful slow jam and cautionary social commentary, the lyrics implore listeners to resist the comfort of complacency and ignorance or pay the consequences:

'Now don't you close your eyes'

The last line best conveys the high-stakes urgency of wokeness. The sense that something terrifying lurks in the shadows.

It's an idea Jordan Peele expanded on in his horror film, *Get Out*, which famously uses the song in its opening scene. Because as the movie made clear — its protagonist slowly becoming aware of an elaborate plot to co-opt his body and trap his mind in an abyss called the sunken place — the consequences of sleeping are indeed horrific.

These examples in tandem solidified woke as the mood of a new era, rising in the aftermath of the modern-day horror story that was the EU referendum and election of Donald Trump, a time when our freedoms can very much feel like they are on the line and in peril. Stay woke. Don't get caught. Don't get hypnotised. Don't close your eyes.

7. Despite what the likes of MTV and Twitter would have you believe, it's impossible to depoliticise woke. Woke, by its very nature, is engaged.

8. The goal is to wake up and then stay that way. As in, be aware and on guard, ready to recognise, call out and actively resist the biases, fake news and inequalities as they come, like the countless members of the Black Lives Matter movement do on Twitter and Facebook, posting smartphone footage of unjust killings, assaults and arrests, sometimes with the hashtag #StayWoke, and campaigning for legislative change. Woke is righteous indignation, backed up by a set of actions as resistance. Woke is serious business. Often said aloud with a raised closed fist reminiscent of Olympians Tommie Smith and John Carlos's famous Black Power Salute at the 1968 Mexico City Games.

9. Despite its changeable nature and twistable journey, woke is inextricably linked with the rise of Black consciousness, which has never ever really gone away

but rather has had surges and swells. This latest wave is most defined by its relationship with social media — specifically, and thrillingly, how Black people have used Twitter, Facebook, Instagram and the like to amplify Black pride and call out systemic oppression. In short, being woke was originally tied to the experience of being Black. But can you be woke and not Black?

10. If you believe BuzzFeed, woke is also the much-needed awakening of the privileged to all manner of societal ills and the willingness to call them out — usually in the form of a white, cisgender, heteronormative man recognising that others who are not white, cisgender, heteronormative and male are often denied equal rights, treatment and pay. See the website's infamous love letter to *Orange is the New Black* star Matt McGorry, a self-proclaimed feminist and BLM supporter. Titled, quite literally, 'Can We Talk About How Woke Matt McGorry Was In 2015?', it was an article remarkably redolent of and created for Internet culture, and one that birthed the phenomenon, #wokebae. And while the hashtag had an expiration date, the meaning had value. Because privileged allies waking up to inequality, speaking out and working to end it is ultimately a good thing.

11. Woke is also actress Anne Hathaway speaking out against the killing of Black teenager Nia Wilson and challenging white people to check their privilege and recognise that 'Black people fear for their lives daily in America.'

12. Woke is also Tarana Burke setting the hashtag #MeToo viral and inspiring hundreds of thousands of women to recognise and voice their experiences of sexual assault.

13. Woke is also a punchline. The wink of an ending to an online joke making fun of the perceived worthy righteousness of woke culture. The stuff of satire, usually said aloud with accompanying gestured air quotes.

14. One must always distinguish between woke as an earnest state of mind and woke as satire. The latter almost always pokes fun at the former. The latter is also the most grating due to its smugness and therefore it is usually unsatisfying. Example: Maroon is just navy red. #staywoke

15. Woke often susceptible to cultural appropriation. Tragically ironic, considering this is one of the very things the act of staying woke would be on high alert against. See woke's journey from Black political circles to white Internet slang via headlines in mainstream media. Also see the *Evening Standard*'s 'woke-ometer', which measured people on a scale of 'asleep' (Theresa May) to 'woke' (JK Rowling)... and included no persons of colour.

16. Woke is not limited to righteous political types. In the Twitterverse, woke has become an awareness of not just racial, political and social injustice, but an awareness of just about anything.

17. Woke, a study in three Tweets, from the earnest to the sardonic:

Another reminder that Trump's campaign is under FBI investigation. Nothing has changed except the media's attention span.#staywoke @RepMaxineWaters

Wake up, sheeple. Bowling Green was an inside job! (inside Kellyanne Conway's head). #staywoke @StephenAtHome

Bill Cosby is just a distraction from Arizona Tea being sold for $1.25 now instead of .99 cents. #staywoke @Phil_Lewis_

18. Not only is woke a political state of mind. Woke has also been commodified. There are woke books and woke movies, woke T-shirts and woke clothing brands. Woke songs and woke dating sites. Woke neighbourhoods and woke vacation destinations. Woke has commercial currency. When Nike featured Colin Kaepernick, the NFL star who protested against police brutality by refusing to stand for the National Anthem during his nationally televised games, many accused the brand of woke-washing, the act of cashing in on social justice. But sales increased and socially and politically progressive people began proudly wearing and showing off their Nikes on social media out of solidarity. And other brands quickly realised you can be political and profitable.

19. Woke also became a form of social currency, a virtue signal on Facebook or Twitter by members of the ever-growing tribe of socially and politically conscious.

But, woke is at its most powerful, and valuable, when it is lived, and not performed. The likes of Martin Luther King Jr, Steve Biko and Angela Davis didn't declare themselves activists. They didn't have to. Their actions did. Woke people know not to and *need* not describe themselves as woke.

20. A random sampling, in no particular order, of additional people and things that are in the original woke canon:

Ida B Wells
Shirley Chisholm
The writings of Zora Neale Hurston and James Baldwin
Black Lives Matter
Barack and Michelle Obama
Sadiq Khan
Erykah Badu
Alexandria Ocasio-Cortez
Rihanna
Stormzy
The film *Queen & Slim*
The Childish Gambino video for 'This Is America'
Gina Miller
Ta-Nehisi Coates
Harry and Meghan
The *Guardian*
Brixton
Harlem
Lagos

Detroit
Grace Jones
Adwoa Aboah
Bob Marley
Vegetarianism and Veganism
The clothes of British fashion designers Grace Wales
Bonner and Duro Olowu
The artwork of Jean-Michel Basquiat, Carrie Mae
Weems, Glenn Ligon, Lynette Yiadom-Boakye and Toyin
Ojih Odutola.

21. Woke has also been weaponised, used in conserva-
    tive media circles as the highest insult, often placed
    within quotation marks, to mean rigid, uptight and
    socially and politically puritanical. When the Duke
    and Duchess of Sussex decided to step away from
    their roles, the *Daily Mail* complained that Prince
    Harry went from 'fun loving bloke to the Prince of
    Woke'. Meanwhile, the HBO show host Bill Maher
    implored Democratic Presidential candidates to 'get
    out of woke-ville' or else lose the election altogether.
22. Woke has been just as weaponised in liberal circles
    as summed up by the BBC's Gender and Identity
    Correspondent Megha Mohan's Tweet: 'Note
    to editor; no-one in diverse circles uses the word
    "woke" anymore. In fact, it's the clearest indication
    of the insular nature of their world if they file copy
    using it in 2019.'
23. Dropping the word 'woke' into conversation among

strangers in a social setting is a pretty easy way to determine where someone sits on the political spectrum without having to invest too much time in uncomfortable debates. Just watch for the nods, stiffened smiles or eye rolls.

24. As various feminists have done with the colour pink, asserting it and the idea of femininity as symbols of strength and power, rather than sexist marketing and naff children's toys, some have attempted to reclaim woke away from Internet misuse, punchlines and clickbait in the spirit of Black consciousness.

25. Wokeness is often twinned with youthful indignation and optimism. See the scores of students who populated the People's Vote March against Brexit in the UK, the March For Our Lives against gun violence in America, and, in reality, the entire history of student protest. Also see the record number of young people who have entered politics in recent years, from Mhairi Black to Alexandria Ocasio-Cortez.

26. Ultimately, wokeness is rooted in love — of self, family, humanity — just as injustice is rooted in hate.

27. Because despite its inherently pessimistic nature, woke is hopeful. To search for Badu's beautiful world requires the belief that one is out there — or at least, capable of being made.

3 WAKANDA FOREVER

Much has been said and written about the fact that social media can make a person feel lonely. But I'd argue it can do the opposite for those who live chunks of their lives in spaces where they are an Only, an experience many Black people are well acquainted with. Anyone who has ever worked or socialised within a setting in which you are The Only One of One, Two, or at most, Three — understands the distinct sense of relief that comes from finally finding a network of people who have lived through similar experiences and understand the particularity of yours. That unique kind of gladness in finding your tribe, people who can be both a mirror and validation of one's difference, as well as providing a kind of encouragement to embrace and celebrate it.

And while studies and polls reveal a loneliness epidemic sweeping through a generation of millennials thanks to social media, it's impossible to ignore how Black Twitter, Instagram and Facebook have heightened a sense of community, connectivity and solidarity for an entirely different demographic, particularly Black people and especially Black women.

In my case, the alternative network I found on social media helped soften the culture shock of moving to a new country until I could find my own tribe on the ground IRL.

As a transplant to the UK, navigating insular, impenetrable circles in publishing and fashion, I have often felt the isolation of life as an Only in a way I hadn't necessarily Stateside. Back home, during my childhood in Virginia and twenties in New York, if I was an Only in the classroom or at work, the extensive tribe of girlfriends I had outside of it all helped fortify me against any feelings of exclusion.

Not to mention I could wake up in Virginia or New York, walk out the door and dive into any variety of enriching Black experiences according to whatever mood I so happened to be in that day. This was something I took for granted, until I moved to London where I found myself in the position of outsider more than not.

In the UK, where I had moved in the late aughts into a historically white, working-class south-east London neighbourhood in the throes of gentrification, I found myself seeking out sameness, in any form, as a reprieve from Otherness. I knew the city had a rich Black cultural scene, I just hadn't discovered how or where to tap into it just yet. During those first six months here, I lived alone waiting for my boyfriend (who is now my husband, and, I should point out, an American mix of Irish and Italian) to tie up loose ends back in the States so that he could board a plane in order to move in with me.

I craved the company of other Americans, people who shared my accent and colloquialisms, people who didn't pepper their spellings with u's or say 'sorry' instead of 'excuse me' as they attempted to navigate crowded pubs and rush hour trains. I formed tight, if fleeting, bonds with people I would have probably never gravitated toward back home in the States, over the smallest Americanisms: a guilty affinity for Chick-fil-A and Ben's Chilli Bowl or subscriptions to *The New Yorker* and *New York* magazine. It didn't take much.

But more than anything, I craved a sense of community with other Black people, specifically Black women, and especially as Black people throughout the diaspora revelled in a new wave of pride and consciousness in the wake of the Obama presidency. I had grown up the product of institutions built to strengthen Black people in the face of systemic discrimination, the child of two graduates of historically Black universities. I understood the power in a strong tribe. And I knew if I was to successfully live in another country, I needed to find a community, even if it meant building one myself. I longed to be in a room where I was one of a loud, rambunctious many — like the greatest of all Black block parties, Sunday dinners, cookouts or family reunions — rather than just the contained, observant party of one.

In the meantime, social media met the need, connecting me with my extended sister circle back home as well as a group of talented Black women writers, early generation bloggers and editors in other cities around the world who I got to know through the Internet. Social media was the thing that tided me over until I could find what I was looking for offline.

I had found small pockets of it in London. At my first Notting Hill Carnival. At the dinner party of a cousin of a friend's friend later that autumn. And at a string of Afro hair salons I tried. But it wasn't until January 2010 that I finally found what I had been looking for on a larger scale.

A friend, determined to show me that London was just as rich in community and melanin as New York (her words: 'if not even more so!'), had invited me to be her plus one for an art party. The Tate Britain had just launched a sprawling, mid-career retrospective of the British painter Chris Ofili's work. Chris Ofili, unapologetically Black and Manchester born, of Nigerian descent. Chris Ofili, Turner Prize-winning member of the famed YBAs. Chris Ofili, the man behind that painting of the Madonna rendered as a Black woman surrounded by big, Black, sexualised asses and actual elephant dung on canvas. The one that offended not just Catholics the world over, but divided the art world and pissed off a fair proportion of the viewing public. The one the mayor of New York tried to ban. Yeah, I'll be there.

It was the Blackest party I had ever been to in London so far, not quite a sea of melanin, but definitely more Black faces than I had seen in a single gathering thus far, beyond my semi-regular trips to Brixton for hair supplies and goat curry. It was 5 February and damp and glacial outside. But indoors, the rooms were warm and the crowd was hot. A DJ played Afrobeat as guests milled around dressed in their finest.

I was buoyed not just by the Blackness in the room — a photogenic mix that included tall, elegant-looking older men in jackets and kente shirts, young, stylish women in clashing graphic prints with all manner of braids and twist-outs, and lean, straight-backed tracksuit-wearing guys with towering, free-growing dreadlocks — but also the Blackness hanging on the walls. Collaged, painted, beaded and gold-flecked odalisques, Black women in regal and sensual repose. A constellation of Afroed heads. Teardrops containing the image of slain Stephen Lawrence. Cut-out images from Blaxploitation films. Ice T. Don King. Blackness was the star, subject and guest of honour at the show.

Near the gift shop, a line snaked its way through the ground floor as guests waited for the artist to sign catalogues and prints.

The mood was celebratory and dazzling. The night felt glamorous, even if much of the work on the walls was haunting and devastating. The evening was a moment and a rarity — a historically white institution and an enduringly homogenous industry honouring the country's most famous Black artist.

But this was a different era to where we are now. Instagram had launched but #Blackexcellence hadn't yet taken off as the natural progression from the Black Power Movement, born in the 1960s, it would eventually become. And I hadn't yet solidified the network of girl-friends I would go on to build following that night — effervescent, ambitious journalists, artists, stylists and executives with thriving careers who not only lived Black excellence but wanted to create space for other women to join them. Women who *did* make space for other women, building out teams, publishing imprints and brands that created new jobs and platforms. I had finally found my tribe! And the shared experience helped minimise the isolation I felt in my work life.

No, Black excellence hadn't yet evolved into a social media phenomenon and cultural sea change. But that was where it had reached by the time Marvel's *Black Panther*, perhaps the decade's most definitive visualisation of Black excellence, beyond the Obama White House itself, hit theatres in 2018.

Like the Chris Ofili exhibition, the *Black Panther* premiere in London had taken place in February. Not that the cold weather stopped anyone from showing up in their boldest, brightest clothes, accessories and African prints. And not since the Ofili exhibition had an unapologetic study and celebration of Blackness generated such fervent excitement among Black folk and the white mainstream alike. Yes, London had hosted the Basquiat retrospective Boom For Real at the Barbican a year before, but that was largely an American show staged in the UK. There was something about the *Black Panther* moment that, like Ofili's evening, felt uniquely British with its cast full of homegrown talent filling both the screen (despite being written and directed by Americans) and the theatre.

My life had changed considerably in the years between the two events. I was no longer a new expat homesick for community, searching for like-minded friends. By that point I had become a part of a large, loosely connected network of Black creatives, many of whom were planning to be at the premiere of *Black Panther* at the Hammersmith Apollo. And when I arrived at the theatre, I realised I had finally found that sprawling, expansive, loud and proud mass moment of Blackness I had been craving when I first moved to the UK.

Outside, the streets were cold and dark. But inside, the venue was alive, every seat full and the walls vibrating with a mix of loud music and animated voices reverberating throughout the space: speaker-shaking bass, Kendrick Lamar's flow and high-pitched 'Ayyyyyeeees!' The audience doubled as a fashion show — all party dresses and heels, statement jackets and sunglasses, conversation-worthy hair and nails.

I had arrived nearly an hour late to find the movie was nowhere near beginning, despite the 7 p.m. start time listed on the invitation. I fell in line with a string of latecomers, climbing the theatre's red-carpeted steps behind a boisterous group of fabulous-looking women including the actress and comedian Michaela Coel. From my seat I scanned the audience and could make out the rapper Stormzy and actor John Boyega, as well as a slew of media peers and friends. On stage, stars Lupita Nyong'o and Danai Gurira stunned in beaded dresses.

The opening scene rolled nearly fifty minutes later. The screen went black, white stars gradually appearing to reveal a dark night sky. A young boy's voice, optimistic and inquisitive: 'Baba, tell me the story of home.' A glowing, blue meteorite emerges from the darkness speeding towards the continent of Africa and landing in a field of baobab trees, as the boy's father explains the history of Wakanda, a technologically advanced African nation, hidden away from white colonialism and powered by the strongest substance in the universe, Vibranium.

Moments later we watch another little boy in Oakland, California playing basketball with his friends unaware that inside his apartment upstairs, his father, an undercover Wakandan agent, is being confronted by his brother, the Black Panther.

Throughout the next two hours and fifteen minutes, the audience whooped and cheered as we watched a film in which Black people are hero and villain, saviour and victim, with complicated paths to getting there. And in between the raucous moments of laughter and applause, we sat in contemplative silence as the film told a story of Africa and Black America, posed questions about Black liberation and Black radicalism and presented the possibilities of gender equity. It was a film for and about Black culture, with a record-breaking $200 million budget.

Few works of pop culture are as widely consumed as the superhero film. Of the twenty-five top-grossing movies of all time, more than half are big-budget, meticulously commercialised blockbuster productions revolving around men with superhuman capabilities. One of the most momentous feats of Ryan Coogler's *Black Panther* is that it takes the globally revered medium and bathes it in Black. It was the eighteenth Marvel film, but the first to star a Black superhero and all-Black cast. The first to be set in Africa. The first Black film of any kind with such a massive budget. It was a movie in which women ran the place, with women warriors and matriarchs saving the day. It was nominated for an Academy Award. And it was the highest grossing superhero movie ever made (more than $1.3 billion globally).

It was also a gift to a global community of people of all races still reeling from the election of Donald Trump two years earlier and the rise of populism — and a gift released during America's Black History Month at that.

Much has been made of all these things. But I was struck most by how the movie shifted the conversation around Blackness away from America (a place that has long dominated the conversation) and became a rousing phenomenon for people of colour everywhere, with social media serving as the Vibranium that powered it.

In the film, residents of Wakanda showed their solidarity by crossing their arms over their heart in salute, a move the director Ryan Coogler styled after, among other things, the Egyptian Pharaohs' burial pose. Years later, some would interrogate the film's mash-up of African references and argue it was a form of cultural homogenizing that did more harm than good. But as we sat in the theatre we were all self-declared Wakandans too — immigrants and expats and homegrown Brits with roots that spanned Nigeria, Ghana, Jamaica, America, Senegal, Bermuda, Trinidad, South Africa, and more. One big diasporic tribe.

In an interview on *The View*, Lupita Nyong'o described it like this: 'Wakanda is special because it was never colonised, so what we can see there for all of us is a reimagining of what would have been possible had Africa been allowed to realise itself for itself. And that's a beautiful place.'

Wakanda demonstrated to many of us what we already knew, that #Blackexcellence exists on a global scale, on screen and off.

To be clear, Black culture has always had currency and Black excellence has always existed. One need only scroll through centuries of history to see this. But I'm talking about #Blackexcellence, the social media-driven amplification and celebration of Black culture. I'm talking about the rebirth of the Black Is Beautiful movement of the 1960s — which was itself an advancement of the Negritude movement of the 1930s that been inspired, in part, by the Harlem Renaissance — as an entirely new era that sat at the intersection of ideology, technology and economics.

This directly impacted my working life. In the fashion world, European brands were casting a multitude of Black models of all skin tones to sell their clothing on a scale the world hadn't seen since the Seventies when designers such as Saint Laurent, Halston and Valentino regularly employed a diverse cast of women of colour ranging from Donyale Luna to Pat Cleveland, Iman and Bethann Hardison.

Meanwhile, fashion magazines began casting Black celebrities as cover stars of big issues in unprecedented numbers, after years of mostly quarantining any woman of colour not named Rihanna or Beyoncé to the smaller 'low risk' issues of the year (January, February and August, for example), indicating that publishers finally viewed them as bankable enough to do so. In August 2018, so many magazines featured Black women as their September issue cover stars that it made global headlines and inspired a wave of celebratory memes. The BBC and Sky News called asking me to comment on this new phenomenon. Major media outlets began referring to this shift, as well as any other wave of inclusion in predominantly white spaces, as the Wakanda Effect.

Wakanda became a synonym for Black excellence and represented all of its possibilities, yes. But it also became a qualifier mainstream media used to reduce the idea to a trend, a fleeting 'moment' that raised the inevitable question: 'When will it end?'

To me, the decisions to feature Ruth Negga, Lupita Nyong'o, Tracee Ellis Ross, Beyoncé, Rihanna, Zendaya, Yara Shahidi, Slick Woods and Tiffany Haddish on the covers of magazines ranging from British *ELLE*, a title I worked for, to *Grazia*, *Harper's Bazaar* and American *Vogue* seemed like a no-brainer. These are all beautiful and accomplished women with a proven track record of appealing to a mass audience. Women who have the body of work, the major cosmetics contracts, the interest of powerful fashion houses — women who tick all the boxes. It galled me that their accomplishments could be reduced to one superhero film.

The impact of the film's enormous success could not be denied, but *Black Panther* was a highlight in a groundswell that had been building for years, rather than the instigator of it. For example, before *Black Panther*, there was *Get Out*, which broke records as the highest grossing original debut ever. The actress, director and screenwriter Lena Waithe summed it up well: 'I think Black people in this industry are making art that is so specific and unique and good that the studio heads have no choice but to throw money at us. They're saying, "How can we support you and stand next to you?" The tricky part is that they want to be allies and they want to be inclusive, but they also want to make money.'

And like *Black Panther*, her 2019 film, *Queen & Slim*, a sumptuous love story and heartbreaking reflection on the politics of Black Lives Matter, written and directed by two Black women, probably wouldn't have been as successful without a global tribe, connected by social media, supporting it.

I saw the film in a special preview in Shoreditch, hosted by BBC personalities Clara Amfo and Reggie Yates. The theatre was filled with London's homegrown Black excellence, most of them women including model sisters

Adwoa and Kesewa Aboah, photographer Rhea Dillon, designer Irene Agbontaen and more. At the end of the screening, guests, eyes wet with tears, all congregated in the lobby for a group, family reunion-style photo, which made the rounds on Instagram in the following days.

It was a moment, and one that was no longer an anomaly in my life. That's mostly because I had long bedded into life in London, and connected with the city's diverse network of Black creatives. What I hadn't imagined, is that Black creativity on both sides of the Atlantic would be as in demand by the mainstream as it currently is.

When we featured Lena in *ELLE* magazine several years before, she described it as a new version of the Harlem Renaissance and used the analogy again when talking about *Black Panther* in an interview with the *New York Times*. 'We're definitely in the middle of a renaissance, make no mistake. In twenty years, people are going to be writing about what you're writing about. But for me, I want more.'

Who doesn't? We all want to see more of ourselves in places where we aren't and deserve to be, whether it be on the walls in a British museum, on a screen in a movie theatre, or in the White House. To find our tribe and rally, arms crossed in salute. Wakanda Forever.

4 AN AMERICAN IN LONDON

It took my leaving America to develop the fullest understanding of my Blackness, womanhood and Americanness, and to see the power in the intersection of those three things.

To be British in America is to be the subject of a mix of amusement and adoration, usually having something to do with the accent and air of civility. To be American in London is to be the object of a mix of scorn, wariness and, at times, reluctant admiration. As an article I once read in *The Economist* put it: 'To be snooty about Americans, while slavishly admiring them; this is another crucial characteristic of being British.'

But to be a Black American woman in London is to be a curiosity. There simply aren't many of us over here. And even fewer on British television screens and magazines. The lack of exposure can either create a general feeling of intrigue or suspicion. This is the case now. And was especially so in those first years of my expatriation, during the dawn of a supposedly post-racial era at the start of my life in a supposedly post-racial city.

Now, as I write, in an age in which identity politics continues to shape-shift, the idea of post-racialism is widely recognised as the myth it is. But in my own life — particularly my years living in the UK, a country seemingly determined not to see race — I've come to realise it's a goal we would all benefit from abandoning entirely. Because the growth isn't in the denying of difference, but in the way we learn to discuss, embrace and live with it, together. Nowhere is this clearer than in the backseat of a London taxi, where I often end up seeing myself through the eyes of others.

My many chats, debates, arguments, recriminations and extended moments of bewildered silence in the backs of cars of British drivers of all races, from all corners of the globe, has contributed to a heightened clarity of who I am in the world.

I arrived in London as 2008 was moving towards its conclusion, a momentous year because so much was rapidly evolving. Lehman Brothers had gone bankrupt sending the global economy into a recession, and Barack Obama had been elected President, giving the world hope for, among many other things, a way out. This was also the year that Fidel Castro stepped down as president of Cuba after half a century in power, the smartphone became a conduit for social media and Beyoncé released the album, *I Am... Sasha Fierce*, which featured among many bangers, 'Single Ladies (Put a Ring on It)'. Things were changing.

I stepped out onto the taxi rank at Heathrow Terminal 5, my skin and senses prickly from the damp chill in the air. I had five suitcases on a trolley. Behind me a family of four strolled out accompanied by porters pushing trolleys with what appeared to be fifteen Louis Vuitton leather suitcases and trunks towards waiting chauffeured cars. Outside, I saw men in tailored suits with Rimowa suitcases, women in burkas with bare-faced babies, teenagers in Uggs and tracksuits, children in Crocs and pyjamas. The world seemed big.

As I took my first taxi ride from Heathrow airport, three things struck me: how unbothered the driver was about getting to our destination in a timely manner, the incredible amount of small talk he was able to fill the incredibly long ride from Heathrow to south-east London with, and the exhaustive detail with which he questioned me about American culture and politics.

What brought you here? Where'd you grow up? Where did you go to school? Where are you going on holiday? Do all Americans take as much vacation as George Bush seems to take? What's with that bloke? Did he steal that election from Al Gore? Why do you even still have an electoral college anyway? Mind, we have Boris Johnson. Bonking Boris Johnson they call him, he's had so many women. It's not right for a married man to carry on like that. But at least he's just the Mayor and not the Prime Minister. Aren't you glad to see the backside of Bush? What about Barack Obama, eh? A smart guy, eh? And

Michelle Obama! Impressive lady. Have you ever met her before? You must be excited about the inauguration with him being the first Black President and all. At least we'll no longer have to hear from Sarah Palin and all those Tea Party types. What a daft woman. Claiming to see Russia from Alaska. No such thing. I've been to Alaska you know. I saw lots of wildlife, but no Russia I'll tell you that. Barack, the best man won. I bet this election must mean a lot to you. I heard he's received a lot of threats. He's got his work cut out for him, that man. But after Bush, the only way is up from here.

By the time we pulled up to my temporary housing — following a slow, circuitous trip through morning rush hour traffic — I felt like I knew everything about the taxi driver's world view and he knew everything that I was willing to reveal about my backstory. Little did I know, this experience would not be an anomaly.

In the London black taxi, I know exactly where I stand, even if I am a paying customer. There were the drivers I met during my first early years as a London resident who all assumed I worked in IT when I'd mention that I was en route to a work meeting. When their grilling revealed that I in fact worked as a global fashion director, they often seemed to have trouble computing the scenario, a fact that still puzzles me to this day. When I asked a former Black colleague about this she explained that IT has historically been a popular career path for Black and Indian professionals in London (I never found any statistics to prove whether or not this is true), a city in which the Black middle class is still a relatively new demographic compared to America.

During childhood, my parents taught me the very American lesson of not discussing religion or politics with anyone unless I was fairly certain the other person believed the same ideas as me.

And living in New York, I learned the very antisocial and yet incredibly common habit of not speaking to one's taxi driver because the driver probably wasn't very interested in speaking to you.

But in London, I have discovered those rules don't necessarily apply. I won't complain about this. I enjoy the little conservational surprises that occur beyond my echo chamber. And I'm a writer, someone who can appreciate a good grilling. In a black taxi, the driver, who must spend years committing the city's entire layout to memory (a literally brain-swelling experience known locally as The Knowledge), is likely to ask you as many questions as a blind date might during a friendly interrogation.

I've spent most of my taxi rides as an expat in the UK defending America to one driver after another — from inquisitive London black taxi drivers in the aftermath of the George W. Bush years to the many outraged Uber pundits I now encounter, weighing in on the latest twists and turns in the tragi-saga that the White House has become under Donald Trump. What I value most about these experiences is that they give me a sense of the realities beyond my like-minded network. And as I write through an unusually polarised election season on both sides of the Atlantic, these kinds of encounters feel increasingly rare and vital. Because how often do we really engage outside of our bubbles of chosen friends and content?

During these fleeting fifteen- to sixty-minute car rides, the questions the drivers ask me are telling. In their eyes, I'm not Kenya Hunt, but rather a representative of one group or another.

To one driver, I represent Americans: *'What's with all the guns?'*

During another ride, I'm asked to speak on behalf of all American women: *'Not a lot of maternity leave over there is there? Sounds like a terrible place to have kids.'*

Or all Black people in America: *'Pardon, no offence but, it looks like Donald Trump really hates people who look like you.'*

Or other Black American women: *'You look like Serena Williams. Have you ever met her?'*

Or Black American women in the UK: *'What about Meghan Markle? Have you ever met her? Why does she have to get all this special attention just for being Black?'*

Meanwhile, the driver is no longer James from Birmingham, England, but rather a representative of something much larger. More than anything, these rides reveal not just what much of the UK thinks about America, but also its assumptions about people who look like me. This isn't the case with all of my interactions with strangers in the UK, mainly because I don't often find myself engaged in brutally honest conversation about culture, politics and world events with strangers. That isn't to say the subject doesn't come up at, say, a dinner party. But I find people aren't generally as forthright about what they really think as I've encountered in the taxi or Uber ride, where a unique and subtle alchemy of conversation occurs between strangers unlikely to ever cross paths again.

There is something in the experience of conversing, for better (enlightening and being enlightened) or worse (correcting conspiracy theories, calling out misconceptions and countering erroneous mansplaining) that makes me even more confident in speaking out.

Recently while discussing Donald Trump's history on race, following some especially controversial comments he made about lynching, a driver pointed out to me that London wasn't like America and that race isn't the issue here that it is there.

'It's because of slavery,' one driver explained. 'We didn't have it here the way America did.'

In fact, I countered, England did. It's just that the vast majority of it existed miles and miles away across the Atlantic, unlike America's sprawling cotton plantations, which predominantly operated on home soil. Both England and America fuelled a slave-owning economy. Both were completely dependent on a slave-owning economy. But the legacy of transatlantic slavery isn't as visible a low-hanging cloud in England as it is in America. It doesn't resurface as plainly and regularly in the school classroom, or over conversation at the dinner table, or on film and television screens as the topic of slavery does in America. But that doesn't mean the problem doesn't exist, or that its legacy doesn't thread its way through the fabric of the day-to-day lives of most Black Brits the way it does most Black Americans. Empire, Jim Crow, whatever you want to call it, the root — racism — was the same.

'We don't see race the same way. Class is more the issue here.'

The driver echoed sentiments I'd heard repeated to me in the office, at dinner parties, at fashion shows and in doctors' offices when the subject would come up. 'It's not the same here, you'll see.'

And to a certain degree they were right.

Throughout history, many a Black American has moved abroad with a dream of living a freer life in a more accepting environment, away from lynchings, segregation and Jim Crow, and decades later racial profiling and redlining. During the World Wars, Black American troops, including both my grandfathers, travelled abroad to fight and protect rights and freedoms they didn't have back home. Experiencing a level of racial tolerance in the streets of France they didn't even know among their own troops, many of them decided to stay. Similarly, artists, performers and writers found audiences abroad were more accepting of their humanity off the stage compared to in the States where singers, dancers and musicians weren't allowed to eat, sleep or even use the toilet in the clubs and hotels where they performed. As Paul Robeson put it when describing his time in Russia, 'I felt for the first time like a full human being. No colour prejudice like in Mississippi, no colour prejudice like in Washington.'

So decades' worth of artists — Josephine Baker, Richard Wright, Langston Hughes, James Baldwin, Quincy Jones, Angela Davis, the list goes on — all migrated to France, while Paul Robeson and Claudia Jones moved to London. (France alone is so rich in Black American history, that the cultural moment has inspired its own wave of tourism.) They all seemed to have the same realisation, that as Baldwin said, America is 'better from a distance... from another place, from another country.'

I had romanticised my move to London, yes. I fanaticised about joining a pantheon of Black writers who cut their teeth abroad in other countries, people like Maya Angelou, Claude McKay and Carlene Hatcher Polite. But my motivations for leaving America behind were different from theirs. I simply wanted to try and see new things, experience life in a different part of the world. Grow. Expand.

Now in retrospect, with the world being in the throes of a peculiar kind of PTSD, one in which identity runs a through-line connecting the cultural and political shifts that caused it, I look back on the why of my move, and the overall absence of race in the equation, with a kind of nostalgia for simpler times. Whether they in fact were is another story. But in terms of my lived experience, they seemed so. My Blackness didn't necessarily inform my desire or need to move elsewhere and expand my understanding of myself as it did with Polite, Baldwin, Hughes,

Davis and so many others. I simply had an opportunity and seized it without much introspection. And I now recognise that as a privilege, a luxury, I was able to enjoy because of the work they put in, creating space in countries, cities and institutions over many decades for the multitudes of Black expats who came after, including me.

It was my life in the UK that drove home my awareness of the spider's web of intersections that define my living. My life up until that point certainly wasn't devoid of racism or sexism. But it took my moving away from the specific ways in which racism and sexism surfaced in America (because before London, I didn't know any different), and discovering more insidious but no less pernicious kinds of bigotry, for me to fully consider the impact discrimination had on me and how life might look without it.

All of this, while digesting the irony of moving abroad to lean in to my growth as an individual, only to repeatedly find myself in situations where I was reduced to being a spokesperson for one perceived demographic or another. Not to mention the obvious paradox in being an American travelling to England, of all places, to search for something more. England. With its monarchy, empire and history of subjugating entire generations of people.

'What are you doing here in London? America is the place to be,' one taxi driver told me in 2011 during a cautious, slow-moving ride home. My adopted city had erupted in riots the day before, as young boys and men — some of them Black and brown, some dressed in hoodies — set buildings aflame following the fatal shooting of Mark Duggan by police in Tottenham. News pundits argued about deteriorating morals and strained race relations. I watched a vox pop in which an older Black woman delivered an impassioned rant on camera, ending the diatribe by announcing that she was ashamed to be Black, while a white news anchor nodded his head solemnly, effectively reducing a complex chain of events to a reductive single narrative. Tottenham had a history of deaths in police custody. Yet the media story had become about gangs gone rogue. And in the midst of it all, a solitary woman taking it upon herself to represent an entire people. Her message: one of shame and self-hate.

Her words contradicted the mood of Black joy and resilience spreading globally as the Obamas prepared to enter a second term in the White House.

Didn't she know? It's a beautiful thing to be Black. As I listened to the cab driver roll out his theory of where London's youth had gone wrong, I thought for a moment that he might be right. Maybe the world had evolved since Baldwin's day, and America was the place to be. Not better from a distance, but on the ground, where killings such as Mark Duggan's were just as tragically common, but counterbalanced by a very loud and organised collective spirit of resistance that was nearly a century old. As the taxi driver wound our way through Canada Water, we could see a car in front of us, filled with four white guys who were squeezed on all sides by enormous Sony TV boxes, brand new electronics presumably taken during a recent round of looting. At a stoplight, they approached two women and offered to sell them one.

'Where to again?' the driver had worked himself up into such a frenzy about the ills of London and why government cuts and gangster rap was to blame, that he had forgotten my destination.

And for a brief moment, I didn't have an answer: 'I guess, anywhere but here.'

Yes, I had romanticised my move to London, but I was under no illusion that the country was a post-racial antidote to the ills of America. As far as I could see the two were different sides of the same coin. And rather than waiting for a time to arrive in which Blackness wouldn't be viewed as a hindrance, I decided to assert it as the bonus I knew it could be, speaking louder and taking up more space as time went on.

Where to? Forward. Always forward.

5 IN MY FEELINGS

Amiri Baraka once described the act of staying cool as: 'to be calm, even unimpressed, by what horror the world might daily propose.' But what happens when the cool exterior cracks and the foundation shakes?

I don't remember much about Donald Trump's Inauguration Day other than sitting and crying in the conference room at work and the feeling of a colleague's hand on my shoulder. The details of that day are fuzzy; I can't remember the content of any of the speeches or what the First Lady was wearing, though as a fashion editor I no doubt had to write about it. I don't remember how many people turned up on the Mall in Washington DC that day, though the figures have been the source of much debate. The only thing I can recall is how the day made me *feel*, how the events reduced me to the ugliest of ugly cries.

I was never a fan of showing that kind of emotion on the job. In fact, when an intern once broke down into quiet sobs during a particularly stressful day in the office, I suggested she hold the tears until she could reach the privacy of a bathroom stall. All this discomfort with emotion, despite my having edited, and even commissioned, stories about the power in showing vulnerability. I didn't walk the walk.

In the conference room that Inauguration Day, I was deeply distraught. From the moment I first set foot in London, my great dilemma was that of belonging. Not knowing whether to move home or stay a bit longer. To wait until my son was school age, until I was ready to move on from my job, until we had had a second baby, until the exchange rate improved, until stricter gun control was in place back home, until the volatile rhetoric calmed down, until we had a clearer idea of how Brexit would look, until the next election year, until the global pandemic subsided, until, until. While some friends of mine had moved abroad, happy to never look back, I was forever sensitive to the pull of home, constantly aware that despite being wildly happy here, I would never belong. And still, Trump's election made it painfully obvious I didn't belong in America either.

My shoulders shook as I tried to swallow sobs and feelings of anger and betrayal: 52 per cent of white women had voted for Trump. 94 per cent of Black women voted for Clinton.

The English adage to keep calm and carry on has always felt uniquely American to me. Underlying the stock image of the strong Black woman is a sense of unwavering calm and unflappability in the face of trauma. And the narratives about us, sometimes authored by us, around the elections played this out. 'Trust Black women', a popular sentiment repeated in news articles and Twitter commentary went. 'When they go low, we go high', Michelle Obama famously encouraged. 'We show up', another popular message circulating on social media said. We show up at the polls where we consistently vote for the Democratic Party, a party that consistently takes Black women for granted. 'We do the work. Why won't America show up for us in return?'

Around this time women's magazines, including the one I worked for, began actively exploring the importance in owning anger, commissioning writers to author pieces about why now was the time to get mad and let the world know about it. I didn't know what to do with my rage, let alone write about it. I struggled to lean in to my feelings and face them. My ability to quarantine my personal disappointments and frustrations for the sake of preserving my mental health had served me well up to that point, whether it was learning how to shut down micro-aggressions at work or skilfully swerving a class-mate's request to touch my hair (something that continued to happen a shocking amount, well into my adulthood).

I knew how not to take the bait. I wasn't the type to easily snap. Instead I'd fold the hurt, irritation and anger up in neat little Marie Kondo-style rolls and tuck them away in the annals of my memory, only to be pulled out when I needed to prove a point. But that felt impossible to do that inauguration day. Years worth of folding, tucking and rolling came undone. And the more I sat with my despair and inspected it, the more I realised what I was feeling was not the kind of anger of women's magazine coverlines and rallying retweets. It wasn't rage at all. It was fear. I was afraid. And no amount of wilful compartmentalising could undo that.

Months before, friends of mine had sent me messages joking that they too would be packing up and leaving America if Hillary Clinton didn't win. We laughed hard and nervously, refusing to think through the inconceivable.

And then the inconceivable happened and I had to face the reality that sometimes optimism and willpower aren't enough and that that was when the real work began.

6 SALLY HEMINGS AND HIDDEN FIGURES

At first glance, the furore surrounding the Duke and Duchess of Sussex's decision to step back from their royal duties in early 2020, and a white supremacist rally in Charlottesville, Virginia in 2017, would appear to be two unrelated events, taking place in different worlds and times. But what both have in common is how they made plain to one segment of society what is obvious to the other: that racism still undergirds the world's biggest institutions, from our governments and schools to monarchies and media. It remains the great unacknowledged elephant in the room, even now when it's discussed more frequently than ever. That's because the discussion rarely seems to yield an appreciation of how the privileged got to that position, and who was oppressed and overlooked along the way – at least, by the people who benefit from racism most. In the case of Charlottesville and the Duchess of Sussex, Black women are central to both.

On 12 August 2017, I woke up to images of white supremacists carrying tiki torches. It was just early enough that the air (it was London's hottest summer on record since 1976) still felt cool. As I clicked through the news alerts on my phone, a tableau vivant of angry white men looked back at me. Eyebrows pushed up, jaws jutting down, chests puffed out. Flames from the torches winding snakelike through the night. Faces exposed for all to see. Sieg-Heiling. Proud.

They were standing on the iconic lawn of my alma mater, the University of Virginia in Charlottesville, in protest of the planned removal of a Confederate statue from the school, which had been established by one of America's founding fathers, Thomas Jefferson. The protest, the biggest and most violent white supremacist rally in recent history, staged at one of America's most historic and picturesque campuses, had made global headlines.

The men wore polo shirts and white button-downs and khakis and I remember being slightly amused by this — the idea of hateful behaviour dressed up in the uniform of Southern American gentility. I rubbed sleep out of my eyes and upset began to settle in. On social media, former classmates, most of them white, posted messages of shock that such a bold act of hatred had taken place at the school, which up to that point was largely known as a utopian academic village. Their messages eulogised a school they thought they knew, a state they thought they knew, a country they thought they knew. Meanwhile, my Black alumni friends were communicating a different message about the protest: 'This isn't surprising or new.'

The cable news networks were playing the protest

footage on a loop. The sheer volume of men was chilling. They had come from all over the world to join in the Unite the Right rally, which had been organised by two alumni of the school. Most had come from Virginia, but a significant minority had travelled from out of state including Ohio and Alaska. It even drew men from Canada, Sweden and South Africa.

And as the world watched the aftermath unfold – a series of violent clashes throughout Charlottesville that left one woman dead – I couldn't help but think the ghost of Sally Hemings, Thomas Jefferson's most prized slave and mother to six of his kids, was watching too.

Much has been written about Sally, and yet we don't know very much about her at all. We don't know her hopes or fears. We don't know her thoughts about bearing her enslaver's children. She left no written accounts. We don't even know how she looked — there are no painted portraits — with the exception of two descriptions of her appearance as 'mighty near white' with 'long straight hair down her back' according to a former Monticello slave. Meanwhile Thomas Jefferson's grandson described her as 'decidedly good-looking'. What we do know has been pieced together from oral testimony about her.

History is filled with Sally Hemingses. Black women behind the white men taking centre stage in history, invisible women with barely a footnote: the labourers who built the landmarks and powered the industries that propped up global economies with their bare, calloused hands. The Internet is filled with modern-day versions of this story. Search the phrase, 'Meet the Black Woman Behind', and you'll find a litany of results: the Black Woman Behind The Green New Deal, The Black Women Who Helped Send America To Space, The Black Woman Helping Starbucks Get Its Buzz Back. The Hidden Figures narrative has played out for hundreds of years. But it's taken on a new tenor as both appetite for these stories, and racial tensions, grow globally. It's hardly a coincidence that the rise in visibility and power of Black women — and people of colour, queer and trans people as a whole — is coinciding with a rise in pushback to all those things.

In a video posted online, in the aftermath of the riots in Charlottesville, one of the organisers of the Unite the Right rally spoke directly to viewers, calling out to those watching from across the world to rally against those looking to persecute white people.

And as his voice rose, his defence growing more unhinged, I felt a growing urge to go home to Virginia, where the racists too felt so at home. I needed to make sense of things in the midst of separation and chaos. And so I did.

Virginia is for lovers. The state slogan beckons, like the cool, blue waves that lap at its coastal edges in hot summer.

When George Woltz and David N. Martin worked up options for the state's new tourism campaign in 1969 — it would be the country's longest-running of its kind — the brief was to attract visitors. Younger ones. New audiences. New generations.

The visual language was graphic and youthful, white words in a serif font and a red heart, all on a black background. The ad team who worked on the campaign had considered qualifiers. Virginia is for beach lovers. Virginia is for mountain lovers. But ultimately decided the simpler road was the best, with no need to examine for subtext. When some assumed the slogan was connected to the Supreme Court case, Loving v Virginia, which legalised interracial marriage just one year before, the founders were quick to dismiss it. Though they did confirm the logo was meant to attract a young generation of visitors to the state — free-loving newcomers in search of adventure.

On the highways that rim the state and inside its airports that serve as gateways to the rest of the world, the logo invites you in, all warm hearts and friendly, slopey a's and o's. It speaks volumes about my parents that I have always loved seeing this sign upon arrival, despite my home's complicated past and my complicated relationship with it.

Virginia. The place where American slavery began. Home to the former capital of the Confederacy. A slice of North America between the Chesapeake Bay and Blue Ridge Mountains. The American South, with all its brutalities. When I went home and drove its highways to visit one family member after another, I was unnerved by how the Trump signs, American flags and gun rights billboards seemed to appear in clusters on the backs of pickup trucks and in the windows of small shops. And yet there are few places I'd rather be. That's mainly because my parents created a different narrative for me there, one that was a safe space of love and family.

My childhood is not without the kind of stories that are commonly projected onto a young Black girl's sense of self. At the age of five, a classmate told me she was no longer allowed to trade snacks with me because her parents found out I was Black. At seven, a white neighbourhood playmate called me a n*gger. I grabbed him by both wrists, swung him around as hard as I could and let go, sending him flying into a bush, the five or six other white and Black kids around me cheering me on. Because, who wouldn't want to be Black?

I'd never experience discrimination verbalised in that kind of explicit way again. But I never quite lost my sense of preparedness for it, like an airbag tucked away inside me, ready to block any blunt force. And I lived in a relatively liberal part of the state, on the coast by the Atlantic Ocean, compared to the parts further west where the politics and culture grew a deeper and deeper shade of red on the electoral map, the closer you got to Appalachia. No matter, those early introductions to racism didn't dim my light. They didn't make me feel lesser than, but rather made me to want to shine brighter.

When I was offered admission and an academic scholarship to the University of Virginia a decade later, I felt a sense of limitless possibility. It was a great school, the top-ranked public university in the country with one of the nation's best English Literature departments, a course with faculty that included a US Poet Laureate and civil rights icon.

Beyond the academics, the school, now 200 years old, is also famous for its storied past and picturesque campus in the rolling hills that approach the Blue Ridge Mountains. Retired, following two presidential terms, Jefferson drafted sprawling plans. The school has the kind of classic beauty that makes it a hit with traditionalists; it's ranked the most beautiful university in the nation and is listed as a UNESCO World Heritage Site and a National Historic Landmark.

While the college's aim was to promote freedom of the mind, what wasn't taught or discussed nearly as openly as the neo-classical architectural feats of the Academical Village, or the high standards of Southern gentlemanly conduct, was that Thomas Jefferson not only owned slaves for his personal use, but enslaved people to build his utopia. Or that following the school's completion, roughly 200 enslaved people worked on the University grounds. Or that within the school's walls, researchers would build the nation's most powerful eugenics programme. 'Even in Jefferson's own imagining of what the University of Virginia could be, he understood it to be an institution with slavery at its core. He believed that a Southern institution was necessary to protect the sons of the South from abolitionist teachings in the North', a report by the school in 2018 revealed.

Not that we needed a report to spell this out. Black students already understood this to be true. And the unspoken truth, only rarely touched on in the odd course here and there, created a general feeling of repression. Beneath the bucolic grounds, running through the raucous tailgate parties with the bow-tied boys and the girls in the floral dresses, the tension between the school's true history and its PR'd one rumbled.

You had to work hard to find the Sallys, the women whose lives were swallowed up by the University. And there were many. I can remember days spent in the old library opening dusty slave narratives in search of evidence of what it must have been like to be a Black woman on those grounds two centuries ago. Many stories wouldn't come to light until long after I left, so many of them involving young Black girls: two students beat and raped a 16-year-old girl in 1826, an incident historians described as unremarkable for its day. In 1850, three students gang-raped a 17-year-old girl. In 1856, another beat a 10-year-old slave girl unconscious. Many of these students were men who grew up on Southern plantations where violence was often considered the only way to achieve and maintain dominance. They carried that thinking to school.

Despite its history, my memories of UVA are largely good ones; a blur of raucous parties and close-knit friendship groups. I navigated the colonial buildings with a feeling that the school was mine just as much as it was anyone else's, even if it wasn't founded with people who looked like me in mind. This was largely *because* of Sally, rather than in spite of her. In my mind, the simple fact that my ancestors quite literally built the place fuelled my sense of entitlement, even when white students would wave the legacy of white supremacy like a flag. Sometimes using an actual flag, the Confederate one, hanging on a student's wall, or once, out of a dorm window prompting campus-wide protest from the Black student body.

Shortly after I graduated, a group of students wore Blackface to a party, prompting outcry. A few years after that, a white student attacked a Black woman running for student council president, telling her 'nobody wants a n*gger for president.' In the weeks before that, she had received threatening phone calls. Incidents like this were also common during my time there. None of these events ever changed the feeling among my network of Black fellow students and alumni that we deserved to be there just as much as our white peers. And none of these incidents seemed to prompt the white student body to consider why this was true. Throughout all the debate and town hall discussions that were the inevitable consequence, Sally remained on the periphery. The more we talked about race, the less we seemed to collectively *talk* about it. So many seemed wilfully unaware of their unearned privilege.

UVA's history isn't unusual. Harvard, Georgetown and Brown University are just a few of the many universities built from the ground up by slaves. And here in the UK, where its history of slave ownership has been largely glossed over, the untold stories of Black and brown bodies behind the gleaming white successes continue to haunt.

As I write, the UK is in an uproar over the Duke and Duchess of Sussex's surprise announcement to retool their role within the royal family into something more progressive. Controversially, they told the world on their own terms, when they were ready, without approval from the crown. In a way, the outpouring of rage — which tellingly has overshadowed far more troubling stories including Prince Andrew's ties to child sex-trafficking, a brewing war with Iran, catastrophic climate crisis-induced bushfires in Australia, and Brexit — has felt just as racially loaded as the rallies in Charlottesville, even if not spelled out as explicitly.

The media has called it Megxit, a term that wholly orients the controversy around Meghan, even though the decision to step back was surely a joint one between husband and wife (Prince Harry expressed desires to leave his royal duties as far back as 2007). And at the heart of the fury, and surely the couple's reason for wanting to step back from their roles as senior royals in general: Meghan's Blackness. Race is arguably the biggest talking point in the story of Harry and Meghan's marriage – and yet few in England seem equipped or willing to talk about it.

Regardless, what's so compelling about Meghan's story is her refusal to occupy anyone's expectation of what Blackness is or what Black womanhood should mean. And she doesn't seem to have any desire to change the opinions of the British public or royal family about her — even though with tabloid headlines claiming she's '(Almost) Straight Outta Compton', and a relative daring to wear a Blackamoor brooch to her first family meet and greet, we know they have more than a few. Much has been made of Meghan's rumoured refusal to be small, fall in line, quiet down, defer to the family. Regardless of her motives, her actions are a powerful thing for young Black women to see.

In a viral listicle titled 'Shit Black Women Ain't Dealing With In 2020', writer Hannah Drake summed up the mood of many: 'Meet the Black woman behind? Nope! Meet the Black woman first! Period!'

While recounting her experience with a racial census in an article she wrote for *ELLE* (and full disclosure: it was a piece that I edited), Meghan talked about wanting to draw her own box, rather than allow anyone to define her identity. She has drawn hers. And most potently, she has dared to do so within an institution as old and rigid as the British monarchy. The world got mad. She took a step back. And moved elsewhere to create a safe space for her family. Let them figure it out.

The ghost of Sally Hemings lives in all corners. She's always there, in both the conspiratorial silence and loud debates. *We* see her, whether the rest of the world is willing to acknowledge the Sallys, and come to terms with the legacy of racial oppression, or not. As I've grown older, I've realised the best thing I can do to honour her legacy in my own life is let go of any compulsion to explain my humanity to anyone who doesn't recognise or value it. I recognise it. I value it. That's what matters most. And the beauty of this moment in history, as Black women rise to the fore, is this overall rejection of personas placed upon us.

I've found myself thinking about Sally a lot since that August morning in 2017. Wondering what she looked like. How her voice sounded. What she would think of this moment we all live in. What she would tell us. No matter how far across the world I drop anchor, the distance doesn't change the reality that I am a product of her, as are all daughters and sons of Virginia. And America. And yes, England and beyond. And I spread out, across the Atlantic, and back again, arms wide, claiming room for myself as I go.

7 UPON REFLECTION

FUNMI FETTO

'Who taught you to hate the texture of your hair? Who taught you to hate the colour of your skin? To such extent you bleach to get like the white man. Who taught you to hate the shape of your nose and the shape of your lips? Who taught you to hate yourself from the top of your head to the soles of your feet?... You should ask yourself who taught you to hate what God made you.'

MALCOLM X.

There is a box. It is tea-stained and tattered because it has travelled and existed for a few decades. The collation of its contents began sometime in the 1970s when it lived under a bed in a small post-war flat close to the centre of London. Soon afterwards it made its way to a West African town and years later it found its way back to

London. Today it is living somewhere in a newly built family house on the outskirts of London.

Inside the box are photographs. A mix of dog-eared black and white and coloured photographs that mark moments big and small in the life of one African family. There are grainy images from a London wedding in the late Sixties or Seventies with Black people wearing perfectly coiffured Afros, bell bottoms, miniskirts and coloured platform shoes. There are pictures of a good-looking Black couple sitting on a sofa in their flat with a backdrop of a mustard print psychedelic wallpaper. The majority of the images however are of children. Happy children. One is a mischievous-looking, wide-eyed Black-skinned girl. There's one where she is wearing a peachy pink-printed summer dress in front of the family car, a baby-blue Volkswagen Beetle, her Afro hair manoeuvred into bulbous twists, her smile beaming into the camera. Another sees her in a playground, carefree, oblivious to the camera, her apple cheeks and sparkly eyes filled with glee. At her fifth birthday party she stands confidently in front of a three-tiered fully iced cake, wearing an equally elaborate pale green-printed Victoriana dress, Black face freshly shined, Afro hair pinned into a puffy halo. This happy girl welcomed the camera fearlessly. She was unaware of the concept and ideals of beauty; what these were, who dictated the terms and who had the means and the power to flourish within it. She was blissfully unaware of what she looked like, how the world viewed her and where her place was in what the world deemed beautiful. She had no idea her nose was flat and wide and a future source of derision and shame in a world where her small, buttoned and delicate equivalents are revered. She had no idea her full lips would be mocked but later desired — only on whiter skin. She had no idea the kink in her hair would draw curiosity and vitriol in equal measure. She had no idea she was Black and that her Blackness would be a barrier to fitting into the social constructs of beauty. She had no idea that there would come a time that what was reflected back at her in the mirror and in photographs would cause her to compare and contrast herself with what the world kept telling her was beautiful. And that she would never, could never, live up to it. But she soon found out. And then she stopped taking photographs. That girl was me.

There are many lies we tell ourselves. I don't think we all do it because we are pathological fabricators incapable of truth. There is a part of us that we shut down because the alternative — whether superficial or serious or something less specific — means confronting something uncomfortable to digest. So we tell ourselves lies. The longer we tell ourselves these fables, the more we recount the stories to ourselves and everyone else, the more we believe it to be true. So it becomes a self-fulfilling prophecy. The box is a reminder of this. For as long as I can remember, I have been saying that I have always hated taking pictures, that the camera has always made me nervous, that the brilliance of a flash and the unmistakable click makes my stomach churn and my heart still as I contemplate the image I will be presented with. But that's not true. The contents of the box prove otherwise. Those pictures are of a girl that trusted the camera without question. She loved to have her picture taken until the world inadvertently told her she had no right to. The term 'she's no oil painting' reminds me that the world has decided what — and therefore who — is worthy to be captured in pictures. Within the narrow confines of what the world generally considered beautiful — a sea of whiteness and the worship of white features — my round Black face just couldn't find its place. I had no idea how long this went on for until quite recently. I was asked to provide a selection of photographs of me between my mid-teens and my twenties. I couldn't find any.

It's impossible for me to pinpoint the exact moment or day or week or year I purposely began avoiding the camera. What I do know now, however, is that this act (an indirect form of rebellion perhaps against the pressures to constantly consider my own reflection) was inspired by a cacophony of obvious and unlikely suspects. The media was one of the early culprits. It had a major impact on my idea of beauty and where I fell in relation to it. Like everyone else, I was surrounded by its messaging, living it, breathing it... Like carbon dioxide. I was totally unaware of the toxic effect it was slowly having on me. Like generations before me I had been indoctrinated to desire 'white-behaving hair'. Women swishing their golden locks in hair adverts made me wish for long, moveable hair — cue decades of burning my scalp with the creamy crack and seeking ever more 'realistic' weaves (Peruvian, Mongolian and Indian) that, ironically, of course never resembled what grew out of my scalp. Women and models I saw in magazines never looked like me. It wasn't just that they were white; their celebrated bodies and features were not something I recognised in Black women around me. Where my dark full lips shamelessly jutted out, theirs were 'cute' rosy pinks that were pretty, polite and restrained. At age 13 or 14 I became slightly obsessed with the shape of Linda Evangelista's thighs, so I spent the best part of a year doing 'thigh trimming' exercises. I also began to dream about having a thinner nose. I was mocked for my nose by both Black and white people. A boy at school asked if the flatness was a result of 'bashing into doors'. He said it looked like a squashed tomato. As soon as I could afford it, I told myself, I would be having a nose job. In the meantime, I had no money so I took homemade measures. I spent hours every week pinching my nose, convinced it would help with the reshaping process. Once I tried wearing a clothes peg on my nose. I discovered my threshold for physical pain was pretty low. As a pre-bedtime ritual, I began to use Sellotape to mould my nose into the perfect shape. In the morning I would stare at the mirror, convinced I could see teeny changes. I imagined how much better my nose — and my life — would be without such a wide bridge. The world would be my oyster! I could be a singer! I could be famous! Every one of my friends wanted to be a singer because why on earth would you want to be anything else? (I hear so many Black school girls singing at the back of the top deck of a bus in the hope they'll be discovered by some bigwig US music producer who just so happened to be taking the 196 bus from Norwood to Brixton Town Hall and I smile wryly. Yes, I used to be you.) My singing voice was at best mediocre — which is why it is so galling when white people assume that being a Black churchgoer means you're a descendant of Aretha. I still cringe at being made to sing 'Killing Me Softly' at the final night of my graduate trainee awayday. It took me a while to admit to myself that despite their cheers and applause, I was dreadful. Yes, there were times I held notes, but mostly I was flat as a pancake. I was never going to make it. Actually, that's not true is it? The inability to sing certainly hasn't held back a good proportion of the music industry. That said, most don't have the darkness of my skin or the wideness of my nose to contend with.

Many discussions around representation and what constitutes beautiful tend to look at the problem as a Black and white one. It is so much more convoluted and layered than that. We as people of colour, even though many of us have been enlightened and educated as to where the self-hate originates, are still so culpable in reinforcing Eurocentric ideals of beauty as legitimate. Many years ago, I met a family friend for the first time. He had only met one of my sisters at that time. My late mother was a very light-skinned woman with thick long jet-black hair. These simple facts meant she was automatically considered beautiful. My sister took after her. (I on the

other hand was a carbon copy of my dark-skinned father).
This family friend seemed almost shocked that I was
related to my sister. 'Yes', a family member agreed. 'This
is the most African-looking one'. The words — which
haunted me for years — rolled out as if it were the most
terribly unfortunate incident to befall a woman. At school
Black girls with 'coolie hair', hair that took on a slight
Indian texture, hair that was not 'tough' and Afro-like,
were immediately deemed more beautiful by Black girls.
I never had coolie hair. Instead I would sometimes draw
the 'picki head' insult. Ironically, these days, because
I wear my natural hair in a slick dancer's bun (helped by
Aunt Jackie's Flaxseed Gel) I have random Black women
telling me I have 'good hair'. At school I would have dined
out on this. Now, it is a term that repulses me. I look at
the Black Beauty YouTube/influencer community. Every
'How to... ' video I have ever watched involves a makeup/
contouring step that thins out the nose. I look at the Black
women that are the most successful and lauded in the
entertainment industry, the romantic leads, the stars of
beauty campaigns and music videos — they are predominantly lighter-skinned and/or have Eurocentric features.
And when we talk about those Black women whose skin,
size and hair — Lizzo, Lupita, Viola — don't fit into the
'norms' of what we've been fed is beautiful, what we say
without explicitly saying it is: 'In spite of your hair, size,
skin colour, you are beautiful, but there is not enough
space for more than one of you in your categories because
essentially you still don't fit THE beauty ideal.' It's the

ultimate backhanded compliment. This mindset filters into real life. There is still no space for a Black woman like me in the traditional constructs of beauty.

That I now work in the beauty industry is an irony that has not escaped me. My job calls for me to think and write about beauty in its most cursory form, as well as to consider its much deeper and layered impact in a way that is not just linked to race. Nevertheless, I am essentially still navigating a world that has long rejected people who look like me – from makeup that doesn't suit my skin tone, to hair products that cannot communicate with my hair type, to sheet masks made for narrow noses... This is evolving, so increasingly I am surrounded by a myriad of beauty ideals. We now have beauty brands spouting diversity, inclusivity, body positivity... They pat themselves on the back because their latest campaign now includes a dark face, someone with non-Caucasian hair, a girl bigger than size zero, a hijab-wearing model... See how forward-thinking we are? Everything's changed! But has it? Sometimes I wonder if this is just a mirage. What the world sees and what the world accepts are two very different things. I have worked and consulted for numerous brands and publications. Unequivocally, the worst-performing images on their social media feeds are those that are as far away from the white and Eurocentric ideal as you can get. So of course their immediate reaction is to park the unappetising images, the ones that give them the least likes, and replace them with the types of images their consumers and readerships prefer to engage with. So for all the talk of inclusivity, there is still an appetite for a certain idealised beauty and I have seen the consequences. I once gave a talk in front of an audience about Black beauty and the issues we as women of colour have to navigate. Afterwards, a young, beautiful, very dark-skinned lady came to speak to me. She was an aspiring singer and told me about the challenges she faced trying to break into the music industry. Despite being a natural tomboy, she was expected to be hyper-sexy and wear weaves, which she said she'd consider if she could overcome her biggest 'problem'. 'I am struggling to cut a break because of this,' she said, pointing to her face. 'My skin is so dark... ' We both held back tears. It was heartbreaking.

Just as I cannot pinpoint when my looks caused me to self-flagellate, I don't remember exactly when I went back to that little girl in the pictures in that box and began to love myself again. The strange thing is it wasn't that I didn't like myself, per se. I had unwittingly separated my outward appearance from my inner attributes so I actually always liked me. I was always confident in my personality. I knew myself to be genial, witty, empathetic, sociable, clever (but self-deprecating — I am British after all), funny, kind, generous, interesting, interested, but also bold, spirited and curious. As a child these latter traits would get me into hair-raising situations — from pretending to be a street hawker in Nigeria to deciding it was 'fun' to run away from home in London. I would always drag my more reserved elder sister along for the ride. Invariably we'd end up in trouble, but boy did we have a blast. As an adult, I am the same, except unlike many of my contemporaries, particularly in the industry in which I work, I haven't needed to take mind-altering substances to be all of these things. But in a world obsessed with aesthetics, these qualities have felt diminished. I've felt like a desirable present that had been packaged in an unappealing box. A gift you can simply re-wrap, but what do you do with a human being not confident in their skin? Yes, ultimately one can consider bleaching creams, hiding under weaves and wigs, forking out for rhinoplasty and adorning oneself with coloured contact lenses (which embarrassingly I had experimented with briefly in my late teens because I considered my brown eyes banal), but where does it end? It doesn't; it's a slippery slope. So my belated process of self-acceptance began with me looking at the inside and working my way out — rather than the other way around. I began to believe the scriptures I had grown up with that told me, 'I am wonderfully and fearfully made'. I began to take pride in my qualities, my character and my gifts. And I began to value them more than the traits I could never have but which the world deemed beautiful. Beauty in itself is fleeting and in its very physical form deserves no accolades — it's no different to glorifying someone because they were born rich. Celebrating someone (or not) on the basis of what they look like has gradually stopped making sense to me. Simultaneously, the rules around notions of beauty are beginning to shift, positively but also negatively (white women desiring and paying to wear cornrows or to own the fullness of our lips and our rears just tells me that the world still won't view a Black woman's beauty as acceptable until the white space gives it their stamp of approval). Regardless of how it moves, however, I've decided to rewrite the rules of beauty for myself so that whichever way the wind blows, I personally am not moved by it.

Now, I'll be honest, it wasn't a snap-your-fingers-and-you're-there situation. It was a process. And I'm not perfect; my relationship with my face is like one of a reformed alcoholic with the spirits that once held her captive. In the past I would eliminate images of myself and for weeks be weighed down by the face that had been staring back at me. In this age of social media where it is almost impossible to hide from a camera, the background noise of my former self rears up on occasion. It reminds me of who, and what, the wider world says is beautiful. It is not dark; it doesn't have a wide nose or a protruding side profile. It is not me. And it tells me I have no right to have my kind of beauty captured by a lens. Back in the day I would have been left bereft, struggling to 'come to terms with my face'. Now? I shut it down and I tell it this: 'I am so much more than my reflection'.

8 MOTHERHOOD

'Now count down from 100.'

It wasn't what I'd envisioned for myself. Lying on a table in a brightly lit room in a women's health clinic on the Upper East Side in New York as an anaesthesiologist held my arm and inserted a needle, calmly instructing me to count backwards. The soft music playing in the background from a sound system I could hear but not see seemed tragically ironic, if not an intentional act of God using the exact medium that would get my attention most: Beyoncé and Michelle imploring Kelly to let a bad situation go. With the exception of two people in the world, no one knew where I was or what I was doing: having an abortion. And yet, I had never felt more seen. I stared at the white fluorescent light above my head and tried to ignore the familiar lyrics and my reality:

'Girl [100] I can [99] tell you been crying
And you needing [98] someone to talk to [97]'

The sound of Beyoncé, Kelly and Michelle's harmonised tough love seemed serendipitous.

'Girl [96] I can tell he's been [95] lying

And pretending that [94] he's faithful and he loves you'

I grew up with a range of motivational maxims instilled in me by my charismatic Virginian mother. They ranged from the Deepak Chopra-esque (during high school: 'reach for the sun because if you miss you'll land among the stars') to Ratchet Lite (when I was climbing the ranks in publishing: 'WERK don't twerk'). Meanwhile, my dad would quietly reinforce lessons around personal finance management and maintaining integrity in school, life and later work.

But there was a piece of slightly less poetic advice from my younger years that stuck more than others: 'Don't mess around out here with these boys and get pregnant.' The message was omnipresent, coming from the mouths of ageing relatives, well-meaning school guidance counsellors and church pastors. There was rarely ever talk about what happens when you do.

For the entirety of my formative years and a chunk of my adulthood, the discussion around Black women and babies was centred around prevention. I'm not alone in this. When a friend told a godmother in her seventies about her plans to have IVF, the reaction was deadpan: 'I didn't know that Black people actually pay people to help them have babies. When I was coming up, everyone was trying to make sure we *didn't* get pregnant.'

The racialising of pregnancy, and the general treatment

of it as desirable for white families and undesirable for Black families, stretches far back, from American government-sanctioned eugenics programmes that saw clinics sterilising women of colour without their knowledge or consent, to the narrative that teen pregnancy was predominantly a Black, inner-city problem. The idea of Black women as hyper-fertile, giving birth too soon to too many babies without being able to afford them, didn't ring true in my world. Instead, the pressing matter was when and how to do it in a way that felt right.

As I write, a petition is making its way through my social networks to improve maternal care for Black women in response to the revelation that due to a range of factors, largely boiling down to institutional racism, we are five times more likely to die from birthing complications than white women in the UK (and four times as likely in the US). We spend so much of our lives trying *not* to get pregnant, that it's not until we're ready for children that we realise the dearth of support systems in place for when things go right or terribly wrong. Or the lack of open dialogue about our reproductive desires. Or the fact that much of the content around our fertility hasn't even been authored by us at all.

Fertility and maternal care weren't on my radar when at 28, my boyfriend observed that my period was late. (It was prone to irregularity ever since I went off the pill, after having read an article about how the hormones could increase the risk of cancer.) I hadn't noticed. With seventeen years on me and three sons of his own, he told me he knew the signs.

A visit to my OB-GYN confirmed his suspicions.

'You're six weeks—'

— I stopped listening. I couldn't bring myself to come to terms with the words that surely followed. My relationship had started as a fling that somehow stretched, on and off, over a large chunk of my twenties. And, like many relationships that occur in one's twenties, it was a learning experience in that it wasn't particularly good for me. All passion, all heated arguments on the phone and in the street and in restaurants, and airports and nightclubs. It was never meant to be permanent, as much as I quietly wanted it to be, despite the dysfunction.

Hardly the circumstances in which to start a family. So I sprung into survival mode, with the goal being to save a life. Mine.

Gauging that the pregnancy news was not what I wanted to hear, my doctor gave me the details for a clinic. I would have an abortion two days later.

I grew up at a time and in a community in which to get pregnant too early, and outside of the safe confines of marriage, was one of the worst things one could do (with falling into insurmountable debt a close second). We worked too hard, our grandparents worked too hard, our ancestors went through too much, for me to miss out on my education and the opportunity to fully explore the possibilities of my future. The phrase 'respectability politics' wasn't yet part of the mainstream vernacular.

The daughter of a stay-at-home mother who carefully considered every aspect of my childhood for peak optimisation, and enthusiastically supported my exploration of virtually every interest (the ballet performances, the painting workshops, the tennis lessons, the Girl Scout trips, the forensics tournaments, the musical theatre rehearsals, the list went on), I grew up with plenty of space to think big. My aspirations were expansive — so many stories to write, parts of the world to see.

I carried this into my young adulthood. I trailed a group of female hunters in Colorado and spent time on a utopian commune in the Blue Ridge Mountains, all on assignment, all with little thought about how overwhelmingly homogenous those scenarios were because I worked hard and had my education and that was the ticket in life.

In my free time I went on ambitious trips when I could afford them: whale shark-diving in Belize, a surf excursion in Costa Rica, beach-hopping in Corsica, and fashion week gate-crashing in Paris. Babies didn't factor in.

So I ruled pregnancy out.

Until it punched me in the gut, literally taking root inside me.

'Some people react like that.'

The nurse said it with a slight shrug, gesturing to the woman hugging, crying and rocking uncontrollably across from me, after the procedure. When I came to, I was sat in a recovery room with three other women in varying stages of post-abortion revival. I had no idea what had taken place before or how I'd got there, who might have wheeled me out of the surgeon's theatre and lifted me out of the bed and placed me in my seat. 'The anaesthesia affects everyone differently,' the nurse explained. She gave me pain medicine and asked me to stay put while they monitored me to make sure I was okay. I stared at the woman ahead of me, who seemed to be releasing all of the emotions I couldn't muster.

I wondered if there was something wrong with me and if that callousness, the absence of emotion, would haunt me. I was a working adult with a promising career, but felt younger, less prepared for the heaviness of the scenario. I was a child of Virginia, a child of the Bible Belt where sex outside of marriage, let alone abortion, was widely considered wrong.

Soon I was bleeding and cramping badly and decided to distract myself from this by checking my phone. My ride, a close girlfriend, was on her way to pick me up. Another girlfriend had checked in to see if we were still on to go to a party in Brooklyn. I had forgotten to cancel. I told her I was ill. When I got home that afternoon I crawled into bed and did not cry, but rather slept deeply and soundly.

The next text message I sent was to my boyfriend, days later, ending the relationship. I didn't want to talk about it. So I quarantined the experience, and the entire relationship really, and tucked it away.

Later that year I began dating someone wonderful and new. We moved to London and got married a year later. A year after that, we had a baby.

'It's a boy!' our midwife said, confirming what we already knew. With breathless excitement, she broke the amniotic sac open to reveal a little boxer's face — eyes, nose and mouth squashed from baby being pushed out. He was born in the caul in a warm birthing pool, two hours after we arrived at the hospital, St. Thomas's, known for its solid ratings and even better hospital room views of the Thames, Big Ben and the Houses of Parliament.

My boy was beautiful and near perfect, smudged face and all. As I held him against my chest, his little legs bent at right angles, resting on top of the milk-padded cushions that had replaced my breasts, I did not think about or imagine how my life might have looked if I'd decided to have a baby that year in New York, rather than here in London with the kind and loving man I had decided to marry.

'This is what we call a failed pregnancy.'

I wouldn't think about that day in the small abortion clinic in the Upper East Side in New York for another five years when I found myself at a hospital in south-east London once again, bleeding, feet in stirrups, staring at a doctor sitting beside my knees, as a hollow feeling spread inside me. She was explaining what had happened inside me. A life and a death. 'A failed pregnancy.'

When the doctor sent me home after scanning my uterus, finding no heartbeat but instead a wilted placenta the shape of an eggplant, and declaring a miscarriage, she told me they would contact me to schedule removal. My husband, juggling our grief with the logistics of lining up a babysitter for our five-year-old son, asked her a series of questions I can now no longer remember. All business, with eyes on the clock, she ushered us out of the room with a 'you'll hear from us tomorrow.' She did not mention that there was a very good chance that my body would not wait that long. And I was in too great a shock to ask her any further questions.

'A failed pregnancy.'

Failed. Failing. Failure. Falling. Later that night, I was tripping down the steps that led into my bathroom and falling onto the floor, where I remained for the rest of the night.

The doctor didn't tell us that my uterus would take matters into her own hands in the antisocial hours of the night, and that the cramps would feel like contractions, so severe I wouldn't be able to stand or breathe. She did not indicate that I might black out from the pain and then gain consciousness again. Or prepare me for that eventuality by sending me home with strong pain meds, or even a pamphlet about which ones to buy and how to mitigate the discomfort at home. There was no preparation. Only a simple 'we'll call you.'

But they never called.

After having my first son, we had waited a while before trying for a second. With no family nearby the cost of childcare felt prohibitive. We debated whether or not our life, our neat, contained unit of three, could stretch emotionally, logistically and financially to include one more.

When I found out I was pregnant, months before my son turned five, I was ecstatic. I had worried it would be harder the second time around due to my being older. When we hosted his birthday party, I had to restrain myself from cradling my abdomen. I felt a constant need to touch my belly as confirmation the pregnancy was really happening. After five years of debating and deliberating over our family planning, the idea of finally having another child felt surreal and thrilling. I was healthy and happy. Grateful. Mentally preparing my mind for the marathon of baby growing and birthing.

My energy level was high. No nausea. No sickness. And my first pregnancy had been relatively smooth and uneventful. So I didn't think anything of the fact that during my final day on a work trip to Paris towards the end of my first trimester, my pee seemed a bit darker than usual. As I boarded a Eurostar train back to London with a colleague and noticed a little light cramping, I thought I'd simply eaten too much crusty bread too quickly during lunch. Maybe the food hadn't gone down well.

It wasn't until halfway through the train ride that I began to notice I was breathing through my mouth as I do when I'm in pain. I felt ill. Maybe the train ride was making me feel nauseous.

But no. A trip to the toilet revealed blood. I was bleeding. Not large amounts, but enough to worry. We were an hour away from London. I was eleven weeks.

So, hands shaking, I stuffed a ball of toilet tissue in my pants and sent my husband a text. I would head to

A&E as soon as my train arrived in London. He would drop our son off with local friends and meet me there, a hospital in a densely populated corner of south-east London because it was the nearest option to where I lived a few neighbourhoods away. 'Are you sure?' my husband asked. It wasn't the NHS hospital where we'd had our first son — a place I had selected because of its strong reputation for maternal care.

When we arrived, the hospital was surprisingly quiet but the wait was excruciatingly long. The hospital was short on staff. A nurse sat me and my husband down in chairs near the doctor's station. A few feet away from my chair, a veneer of dried blood stained a stretch of floor like some kind of morbid watercolour. No one seemed to notice. When I pointed it out, a nurse apologised and paged the cleaning staff. We moved to a different corner of the room.

Thirty minutes later, the blood still hadn't been cleaned up. If I'd had the presence of mind, I would have taken that as a sign and left. But it was late and I felt too unwell. An hour later, I was called into a small room only to be asked to wait longer. Roughly four hours after we arrived, a doctor examined me but could not make a definitive call on whether or not the pregnancy was still viable. So he sent me home and asked me to return in a few hours once the early pregnancy unit opened at 9 a.m.

As my husband and I sat in a crowded waiting room that next morning I tried not to cry as I read the literature taped to the walls, posters telling women where to go, who to see and what number to call should they have a miscarriage.

I was surrounded by Black and brown women, including a teenager with a bulging belly sat next to her mum. A woman in a burka struggling to keep three rambunctious children quiet. And a young Caribbean-sounding woman dressed in a work uniform sat on her own.

As we waited, a midwife chastised another for showing up to work late. In another room, we could hear a woman sobbing loudly.

Have you recently suffered a pregnancy loss? a poster asked me from across the wall. It seemed irritatingly presumptuous.

But the words stuck and surfaced later that year when I had a second miscarriage.

'There were two. I'm so sorry,' a doctor told me.

Two. Twins. Two sacs. So small. Too small. No heartbeats. One gone at seven weeks. The other at ten.

I found out about my second miscarriage two days before Thanksgiving. After the trauma of the first loss, I had decided to go with private healthcare for the early scans. If all looked okay, I would share the good news with our families by Christmas.

But things didn't look okay. I'd walked into the hospital thinking I was literally full of life, but the scan instead revealed a graveyard. What was once growing and alive was now disintegrating tissue matter. The doctor explained my options and then supported my decision to book a surgical removal right away.

It was difficult for me to see the situation as anything other than a death. And one that took place inside of me, twice. Twins.

We were scheduled to host a Thanksgiving dinner of twelve friends and family, some of whom had travelled from the States and were staying with us. It seemed too late to cancel. And I didn't want to answer anyone's questions or talk about it or listen to comforting words. I needed the distraction. Better to just keep quiet for the moment and cry it out later.

It had dawned on me that I had spent a fair amount of 2017 trying to get pregnant, pregnant, or losing pregnancies. And it had been a very bad year as a whole with Brexit and Trump-induced angst spreading a cloud of funereal unease. There was the unpredictable economy, damning environmental news, growing xenophobia, a spike in hate crimes, and increasingly polarising and vituperative political rhetoric. My family dog back in Virginia died. And Borough Market, a local haunt my husband and I felt a special connection to, made international news when a group of men drove their van through crowds of people before randomly stabbing victims in a terrorist attack. That night, I could hear the sirens of ambulances and fire trucks rushing through my neighbourhood towards the scene of the crime. Weeks later, seventy-two people died in their homes when Grenfell Tower, a block of council flats in North Kensington, erupted in flames. And weeks after that, I lost a baby.

As far as years go, 2017 was a personal low. And waiting in a hospital room, trying to swallow back tears as a doctor explained to me what the procedure would involve, felt like my rock bottom.

The thought of drowning my depression in a plateful of pumpkin pie while surrounded by people who could divert my attention away from the source of it, seemed like the way to go.

'Are you okay?' the doctor asked me the next day as I sat in a hospital gown listening to the anaesthesiologist's instructions.

'I'll be fine just like every other woman who has gone through this. I know these things are very common,' I replied.

'It doesn't make it any less hard,' he said with a sad look on his face.

When I came to an hour later, I felt like I had just woken up from a long night's sleep, wide-eyed and alert. Less woozy than I was during the abortion in New York, but much more sad. Devastated. Distressed that my body was failing me.

That night I went home and peeled potatoes. The next day we held the dinner as planned.

After our family members returned to the States following Thanksgiving, I became prone to crying in a way I never had before. I worried that my son — so perceptive, so attuned — could sense that something was wrong. My husband surely did.

I wondered if the unwavering resolve, the stoicism with which I'd handled the abortion all those years ago, had backfired. My usual optimism and pragmatism was failing me. I was disappointed. Angry. Unsettled. And unsure of myself. I began to second-guess my everyday decisions in a way I never had before because the decision-making that led me to this point hadn't worked. I thought about all the things I did during that year of loss: a promotion at work and business travel to Paris, Florence and Tokyo among others. Those were things I had wanted but did they come at a price? I wondered if the narrative I had always resented and dismissed as archaic, the idea that a wife and mother always had to choose between work and family — never both — might have credence.

While all of this was happening, a conversation was growing around the abysmally poor maternal health outcomes of Black women in the US. The American non-profit media organisations ProPublica and NPR had published a report revealing that Black women were dying from pregnancy-related complications at a rate that rivals developing countries, and that Black infants in America are twice as likely to die as white ones. Even more revealing was the fact that Black college-educated mothers who gave birth at local hospitals were more likely to suffer serious pregnancy- or childbirth-related complications compared to women of other races. The same went for women with financial means. Black middle-class women were more likely to die from childbirth-related complications than white working-class women. Rich women were also not immune. Beyoncé Knowles gave an interview to *Vogue* revealing her own struggles with pre-eclampsia, which Black women have a higher risk of developing. And Serena Williams gave an interview to the same magazine about how she nearly died in childbirth because the medical staff ignored her requests for a CT scan.

'It tells you that you can't educate your way out of this problem,' Raegan McDonald-Mosley, chief medical officer for Planned Parenthood Federation of America, told ProPublica in 2017. 'You can't health-care access your way out of this problem. There's something inherently wrong with the system that's not valuing the lives of Black women equally to white women.'

The *New York Times* attributed the problem to the 'lived experience of being a Black woman in America'. But I lived in the UK, where it was apparently just as bad, with Black women having a fivefold higher maternity mortality rate, though this discrepancy wasn't quite as openly talked about. No matter which side of the Atlantic, it was clear that race often impacted not only how a patient was perceived but the kind of medical care she would receive.

And as I looked back on my abortion, childbirth and miscarriage experiences, which spanned plush private hospitals to poorly funded public A&Es, I couldn't help but wonder: if I were white, would I have gotten a more thorough explanation of how my miscarriage would look before being discharged that day in south-east London? Would I have received proper follow-up and after-care, or even a phone call? And if the council were a wealthier and whiter community, the hospital would be more adequately staffed.

As women back home began to open up about their own complicated stories it inspired me to start telling friends and strangers about mine as a form of therapy, but also as a way of finding out if my experiences might be related to a bigger problem. The act of talking about the losses with other women itself became a form of healing. Friends and peers began to tell me about their own disappointments and heartbreaking experiences: the friend in south-west London who endured eight miscarriages before successfully having a baby boy with the support of a doula; the friend in Virginia whose doctor ignored her complaints that her labour pains felt unusually severe (she nearly died in childbirth); or the colleague who had multiple failed rounds of IVF.

The healing for us all was in the stillness of rest and recovery and the passage of time, yes, but also in the talking and sharing.

In her 1988 book, *A Burst of Light*, author Audre Lorde discussed the act of self-care decades before it became a social media moment attached to millennials: 'caring for myself is not self-indulgence, it is self-preservation, and that is an act of political warfare.'

'It's time to push.'

I had my second son in 2018, a good two years after I had envisioned it might happen. There we were, in the same hospital overlooking the Thames, Big Ben and the Houses of Parliament. His little face squashed. I pushed him out in a birthing pool of warm water with the aid of a team of midwives who helped me have the natural delivery I wanted after refusing to allow any medical interventions.

Unlike my experience birthing my first son, my second labour felt like one long contraction, my body rejecting coaching from any voice but the one inside my head. The midwife didn't have to tell me when it was time to push, I already knew.

I screamed my son out, hollering with each push. Screaming for the twins I said goodbye to on Thanksgiving Day. Sobbing for the child I lost during that train ride from Paris. Yelling in release, relinquishing all guilt over choosing my life above any other that might have stunted it all those years ago. And crying with relief at the sound of a healthy pair of lungs, a tiny yowl cutting through the air.

9 SKINFOLK

Are skinfolk always kinfolk? As the world recognises us in unprecedented ways thanks to the galvanising capabilities of social media, and as the world of culture rushes to capitalise on that moment, showing Black people on film, TV and the glossy page, the question underpins the movement.

I had never heard of the term 'diaspora wars' until a few years after I moved to London, as Black Twitter was becoming a cultural force. It was here that I began learning about the real nuances of cultural difference. Through dinners with newfound friends from Brixton, Lagos, Kingston and Johannesburg, I discovered the light-hearted inside jokes and more passionate arguments about origin, ownership and belonging that would often turn a dining table or social media feed into a virtual Armageddon. I listened quietly to fiery deliberations about the critical regional hierarchy of jollof rice, the merits and drawbacks of Woḷé Ṣóyinká's 'Tigritude' and the African-American community's perceived obsession with Blackness.

Are skinfolk always kinfolk? The saying I had often heard back home in the States took on a new meaning here. The debates exposed a landscape that during the best of times seemed diverse and during the worst, divided.

I largely navigated it with my eyes and ears wide open and my mouth shut, mainly because my experience and point of view up to that point in my life was so oriented around America. And also because the sight of these debates made me uneasy, like watching cousins break out in a fistfight during a family reunion, knocking over the potato salad and decimating the pound cake.

In Chesapeake, the coastal town in Virginia where I grew up, Black meant the descendants of African slaves. We studied colonialism and the Civil War in school and took annual field trips to Jamestown, the first English settlement in the Americas, which was just a short bus ride away. I grew up a forty-minute drive away from Point Comfort, a sandy stretch of the Virginia Peninsula where an English ship containing '20 and odd Negroes', men and women who would become the first enslaved Africans in the English colonies, landed 400 years ago. As a child, the history and legacy of slavery cast a shadow over everything. And because of its sheer magnitude, spanning continents and centuries, I assumed Blackness, the core of it, meant the same for everyone.

I grew up reading Black American women writers, to supplement the Mark Twain, William Faulkner, Tennessee Williams and William Styron we read in school. Women like Zora Neale Hurston, Ida B. Wells, Maya Angelou, Ntozake Shange, bell hooks, Toni Morrison and Alice Walker — storytellers who largely centred their stories around the Black American experience, which was inevitably linked to the legacy of slavery.

I was raised by two parents who came to adulthood in the age of 'Black Is Beautiful', an American movement that itself was a corrective against the many false narratives (Black is lazy, criminal, hypersexual, dysfunctional, the list goes on) borne out of slavery.

Admittedly, as a child, the depth of my knowledge of African history was shallow: Nelson Mandela and South African apartheid, which echoed American civil rights history (always circling back to the States), and, thanks to pop music and MTV, the hunger crisis in Ethiopia.

Even during my time at university, my experience of Black culture beyond America was narrow outside of a few courses that touched on diasporic studies, and a cluster of friends from Ethiopia, Nigeria and Haiti. I went to college in the South, where all-American sorority and fraternity culture, both white and Black, dominated the campus culture.

It wasn't until I moved to New York, developing close friendships with women and men from places as far-ranging as Grenada, Nigeria, Jamaica, Ghana, Togo and Zimbabwe, and later settled into life in London where my Black American womanhood made me an Only in most settings, that I realised the Blackness I lived was very much an American construct.

This seems especially pertinent now, a year after the 400th anniversary of the first African slaves setting foot in the Americas. Many Americans, Caribbeans and British have been travelling back and retracing their roots, inspired by the Year of Return, a campaign Ghana's President Nana Akufo-Addo declared, to unite African descendants the world over.

In *The Black Woman*, an out of print anthology published in 1970 that has since got a second wind in the age of Black Girl Magic and Instagram, the author Fran Sanders writes:

For years, the white man has projected the theory that all Black people were the same. The outside person may change in size, shape and, to a certain extent, color. But on the inside was contained an admixture of slyness, laziness, amorality, stupidity, dishonesty and on top of this was added the ability to shuffle along under the worst of life's circumstances and remain happy-go-lucky. He was wrapped up in a tight little package and neatly disposed of, thereby eliminating the necessity of dealing with him. But that was light years ago and I am optimistic. The Black man means to be seen and heard. And indeed he is. But what of the Black woman? What has become of her?

Sanders next lays out an extensive examination of age-old misconceptions of the Black woman as 'conversation pieces or interesting oddities', 'castrating matriarchs', or 'hot-house lilies':

Certain fixed notions are uniformly projected onto the Black woman regardless of age, background, personality, education, ability, etc. All of the notions are those which caused women to chafe under the yoke of Victorianism. We must constantly prove ourselves. It is not enough to be good at something or to be capable at our jobs or to have very valid thoughts on any matter at hand.

And while much has evolved in the decades since the publication of her essay, many discussions around Black women — and Black people in general — still largely centre around correcting misguided perceptions the white audience has of us.

This is tiring and as Toni Morrison rightfully pointed out in 1975, a distraction that 'keeps you from doing your work.'

It keeps you explaining over and over again, your reason for being. Somebody says you have no language and so you spend twenty years proving that you do. Somebody says your head isn't shaped properly so you have scientists working on the fact that it is. Somebody says that you have no art so you dredge that up. Somebody says that you have no kingdoms and so you dredge that up. None of that is necessary. There will always be one more thing.

Like the Black man of the 1970s Fran Sanders wrote about, the Black woman of 2020 means to be seen and heard. Indeed, we are much more than that. Such is the proof of progress. But in light of this, any talk that involves correcting age-old stereotypes and misconceptions now feels like a time-consuming step backwards. To take on the role of educating one's classmates, colleagues or neighbours about what it means to be Black is to participate in the narrative that we are one thing, that one voice can speak for us all. When in fact one voice can only speak to the particularity of one's truth.

The same can be said of the misconceptions we have of each other throughout the diaspora. What are the differences that divide us and what are the ones that bind?

These were the questions that fuelled flash fires of enthusiasm, outrage, and outrage about the outrage that erupted after Focus Features released the official trailer for the film *Harriet* about American abolitionist and political activist Harriet Tubman in 2019. It set various corners of Black Twitter alight with arguments about the director's decision to cast Cynthia Erivo, a multi-award winning British actress born to Nigerian parents, in the title role. 'This is a slap in the face', one Tweet attributed to a growing movement called American Descendants of Slaves. 'We can't tell our own stories?' It echoed similar statements made when Jordan Peele cast British actor Daniel Kaluuya as the lead in his horror film critiquing race in America, *Get Out*, when Ava DuVernay cast David Oyelowo as Martin Luther King Jr in the historical drama *Selma*, and even in Spike Lee's television series *She's Gotta Have It*, when Nola Darling complained to her British Nigerian lover, Olu, that British actors are 'taking all of our roles'.

The diaspora wars had spilled over into pop culture and the central issues seemed to be the many meanings of

Blackness and who understood which kinds of Blackness best in order to authentically portray them.

Erivo responded:

'Actors are free to go where they please for their work, but I dare you to do that fully as a Black woman in the UK. If I see it, I applaud it …What was for someone else was never mine in the first place. Please believe that I have turned down roles I know I have no business playing. This role is not one of them… If you met me in the street and hadn't heard me speak, would you know I was British, or would you simply see a Black woman?'

Later, in the weeks leading up to the film's release, she elaborated: 'I get that there is upset for me playing this role, and I understand where it comes from. It comes from so many African-American women feeling that they don't get seen… There isn't enough — nowhere near enough — for us, as women of colour, to see ourselves. And so I understand why this particular role, which is held to high esteem in this community, feels like it's losing one of their own.

'But at the same time,' she continued, 'I would speak to it as a woman of colour. The only way we can come to agreement or to a common place is to understand that we all have suffered from feeling invisible; we all have suffered from otherness. And the only way to combat that is not to separate each other from each other, but to come together and have that discussion and understand what that is.'

We know that American actors have played their share of African roles, among them Forest Whitaker as Idi Amin in *The Last King of Scotland* and as the spiritual mentor Zuri, in *Black Panther*, or Don Cheadle as Paul Rusesabagina in *Hotel Rwanda*. But it's worth exploring Erivo's point. Skinfolk. All united by the legacy of colonialism, all divided by the displacement that the transatlantic slave trade wrought.

To focus on our differences rather than learn from them is to fulfil the promise of transatlantic slavery to divide and conquer. It's to pit ourselves forever at odds with each other, over who is Black enough, free enough, human enough — that very same distraction racism presents.

Not to mention the argument against Erivo portraying an American slave works under the assumption that only Americans know racism. It may not surface in the same way, such as through a hateful comment on the New York subway or a Confederate flag sighting on a road trip in Virginia, but it's there. One need only look at the stories of Windrush and Grenfell to know this.

I've realised that I gain much more from examining the perceptions we have of each other, individuals throughout the diaspora, and using that understanding to build each other up.

On the cusp of my final year of university, during a summer internship in New York, I met a girl named Nana. Beautiful and impossibly stylish with model-long legs that she normally kept covered in vintage jeans, distressed to just the right point. She wore cornrows that traced neat parallel lines down her scalp. American, she was born in New York, raised in Accra, schooled in the mountains of central Ghana as a boarding student and regularly flew to England to visit extended family. She was well travelled and worldly.

On the surface we may have looked similar, two lanky brown girls interning at the New York alt-weekly *The Village Voice*. But our lives, our childhoods, our families and cultural references could not have been more different. She grew up in New York in largely Black immigrant communities before her parents sent her to their native Ghana where her family had drivers and household staff. Meanwhile, my world was one of American public schools, car pools and weekend chores in Chesapeake, Virginia. And through these differences, Nana offered me a new image of Black girlhood and what we could be — and showed me the value in seeking out a diasporic network of women in my own life, women who could help me interrogate what I had been taught, and challenged me to leave my comfort zone and explore geographically new environments. As we've grown older together as friends, I can look back and see how Nana's free and open approach to travel contributed to the making of me.

When she and I planned a girls' trip to Corsica in the summer of 2007, we attracted the intrigue of locals who weren't accustomed to seeing Black women on the island who weren't prostitutes. When they looked at us, walking together in our bikini tops and shorts, arms full of magazines, books and rolled beach towels, living our best lives, they surely did not see an aspiring journalist from Chesapeake and a budding novelist from Queens, or a descendant of American slaves and child of Ghana. They saw two Black women. 'The only Black women we see around here are on the music videos on TV,' the owner of our hotel admitted to me. I was too happy to be on vacation with one of my closest friends, skinfolk and kinfolk, heading out for a day of luxuriating on a boat in the Mediterranean and talking about life, love and writing, to care what he meant.

10 MAKE YOURSELF AT HOME, BUT NOT HERE

I just wanted to book an Airbnb. How difficult could that be? A series of rejections waiting in my inbox was my answer.

'Helen is unable to host your stay,' the first one read.

This was surprising. The property was listed as being available. All of the Airbnb listings in my search results were. A 'HUGE, luxury' two-bedroom flat in Dulwich. Semi-terrace half-houses in Forest Hill. A-one bedroom in Peckham. All available, until they weren't.

There was the woman whose 'sprawling, trendy flat, one-minute from the train station' was listed as being free for the entire month of February. But when I submitted a request to reserve the place, she denied it and sent a chipper rejection: 'Sorry but I don't know the dates I'll be travelling that month. Hope you find somewhere!' The cheeriness of the 'hope!' and the undercurrent of something decidedly much less cheery, stood out to me as prophetic, which of course it was.

Next, the 'large, slick, modern family home'. 'I can't

do those dates I'm afraid.' She suggested dates beyond my window.

And then 'the house with fantastic views of London': 'Our house isn't available on those dates. We should have blocked out the calendar!'

Airbnb profiles require a headshot, inviting the kind of snap judgments that fuel online dating apps like Tinder, Grindr and Bumble. My photo was polished and pleasant: me smiling in Comme des Garçons stripes, naturally lit by the sun, my skin unambiguously Black. My name, an African country. Extra Black.

I was no stranger to the experience of Black paranoia, a uniquely pernicious kind of suspicion in which the lived experience of discrimination makes you highly attuned to it, no matter which end of the spectrum the bias falls on. I knew there are no interstices between unconscious bias and racism, which exist in unison as one big crag and tail. My alarm bells were sounding.

I tried requesting one more booking as a test — a 'gorgeous flat with a HUGE garden' — located just down the road from where I live. The rejection came quickly: 'We're having work done on the place that month. We should have blocked out the calendar, sorry we can't help you!'

I was dismayed. Having spent a chunk of my adult life writing for publications with large readerships, I was accustomed to brands asking me to stay in some of the best hotels in the world in exchange for my published opinion of them. I've stayed in lavish five-star hotels in Paris, New York, Los Angeles, Rome, Florence and Kyoto to name a few. It shouldn't be this hard to reserve a flat in Peckham.

If one were looking for a clearer example of the fallacy of respectability politics, one need look no further. No number of degrees or impressive job titles will protect you from the damning sting of a surface judgement.

I was looking to book in late September, hardly high tourist season. The schools would be back in session. Not to mention that the neighbourhoods I was seeking were well off the sightseeing path.

The occasion was my parents' upcoming arrival to visit their soon-to-be born second grandson. Their trip would be several weeks long. So it seemed more sensible to rent a flat local to my house. After full days spent helping us with the baby, I wanted them to be able to retire to a space of their own where they could have a good night's sleep, rather than have to deal with both jet lag and the round-the-clock crying a newborn might bring.

I had heard booking while Black could prove tricky. A close friend from Detroit once asked me to write a testimonial for his Airbnb account, attesting to his good character and legitimate line of work, in much the same way people might post glowing words about a Chinese takeaway on Google Reviews. My friend was a handsome actor with a steadily growing IMDb CV, a frequent flyer who was having difficulty finding a place to stay during his upcoming holiday in Madrid. I balked at his request ('Does this not feel desperate?'), but agreed. It reminded me of my years dating in New York, all those nights in which I'd have to be the one to hail the cab because yellow taxi drivers rarely ever wanted to stop for Black men.

'Could you be sure to sign the testimonial off with your work title?' my friend asked me. 'That will look more impressive,' he said. I brushed it off, not realising that without the recommendation, his attempts to find lodging would probably be in vain.

This memory fresh in my mind, I sent a message to the last of my rejecters out of curiosity: 'I'm sorry to hear the place is now unavailable. If the circumstances change, please let me know.' I signed the note with my name and job title. Minutes later, I got a response: 'Give me 24 hours to try to make this work.' And just like that, the 'work' scheduled to be done on the home was no longer an issue.

I could only assume that my alliance with a powerful magazine and/or a quick Google search had assuaged any reservations the owner initially had about accepting my booking — and that whatever those original concerns were, they had been related to my appearance. Specifically, my skin tone (because what else could it be?) In short: an old problem, on a new platform.

I didn't follow through with the booking out of principle. But the indignation stuck.

I'm accustomed to seeing bigotry online. Usually it comes in the form of inflammatory social media comments attached to ambiguous profile photos, viral video clips of white people calling the police on Black people for essentially being Black, while earning nicknames from Black Twitter like 'Permit Patty', and, increasingly, from the mouth and Twitter account of the President of the United States. But this kind of racism is often consumed at a distance and positions us as witness, rather than direct recipient. But with Airbnb the perpetrators aren't anonymous or sequestered behind a shield of Secret Service men and White House walls. With Airbnb, the perpetrators are visible, smiling with nice homes. Homes into which they're waiting to welcome complete strangers with open doors — as long as those strangers aren't Black. As long as those strangers aren't me.

The Airbnb rejections also heightened the reality that racism is all around us. Because if that is the case online, it must also be so in real life. The polite swerves don't just come from nowhere, they come from the attractive five-bedroom house down the road from where you live, or the apartment building on a neighbouring high street. Or the lovely seeming people you wave hello to on your way home. Or the friendly looking couple standing across from you on the train platform during your morning commute to work. People with clearly drawn boundaries that fall on racial lines. Not all people. But enough.

Just months before, Airbnb was under fire when a host kicked five Black men out of her New York townhouse. A video that travelled quickly shortly after it was filmed and posted online shows the woman, 'Kate', asking her unwanted guests: 'Which monkey is going to stay on the couch?'

One of the guests, Kenneth Simpson, was understandably dismayed. 'I thought, is this where we are today? We made a point that we're educated, working professionals. And it doesn't even matter if you're an educated person, because no one deserves to be called a monkey and be dehumanised for no reason.'

He said it particularly stung because Kate was Asian, an ethnicity also prone to being on the receiving end of Airbnb rejection. When a law clerk named Dyne Suh tried to rent a California cabin via the website, a host cancelled it several minutes later. 'I wouldn't rent it to u if u were the last person on earth,' she wrote before adding, 'One word says it all. Asian.'

When a news network later interviewed Suh about the incident, she was teary: 'It stings that after living in the US for over twenty-three years this is what happens. No matter if I follow the law ... no matter how well I treat others, it doesn't matter.'

Her words were about America, but the snubs here in the UK felt familiar, if a touch subtler.

But regardless of geographic location, Airbnb created the illusion of freedom and democracy, even if inequality snaked its way through the information architecture. Make yourself at home — just not our home. We're booked. We cannot host your stay.

This is surely a parable of our time.

11 I SEE BLACK PEOPLE

I remember a late summer walk with my seven-year-old in which we were heading to our neighbourhood bookshop, a local gem of a place known for a brilliantly edited mix of inclusive titles such as *Julian Is A Mermaid* and *Woke Baby*, dedicated to raising 'equality in children's books'. There, we bumped into a mix of friends as we usually do – all shopping with their kids for birthday presents for one child's party or another. As my son and I walked home, a giant open-top, double-decker party bus cruised by, revellers dropping it like it's hot to a kind of Christian dancehall music blasting from the speakers, encouraging passers-by to 'Praise Him' and 'Trust Him'. An elderly woman walking in front of us stopped to dance along, waving her cane in the air towards the Christian partiers and smiling. The chants and cheers from the party bus got even louder at the sight. The elderly woman was all bent knees and swaying hips and waving cane and 'aaaayyyeee'. The Christian partiers were all popping booties and shaking shoulders and waving hands and 'hallelujaaaaaah' in response. My son stopped and watched it all, head tilted to the side, his hand clutching mine.

'Mumma, why are all of those people saying hallelujah?' he asked.

'Because they want to invite people to come to their church, lovebug,' I responded.

He continued, 'And why is everyone on the bus Black?'

I paused. 'I think it's because it's a Caribbean congregation, dumpling,' I added, reading the ministry's name on the side of the bus.

His curiosity wasn't satisfied. 'Why is the Caribbean filled with Black people?'

I tried to answer his question as best I could, touching on the Atlantic slave trade and the African diaspora in a way that a seven-year-old might understand. And then we walked in silence for a few minutes as I gave him the opportunity to digest it all. 'Do you understand, sweets?'

He let go of my hand and pointed his finger. 'I don't know what you just said about Black people. But there's a dead pigeon. Can we talk about that?'

The moment also reminded me of another late summer evening stroll about ten years ago when I was walking through the Upper East Side in Manhattan, hand in hand with an ex-boyfriend. We were ambling behind an attractive family of three, a little red-haired girl who couldn't have been older than three or four, holding mom and dad's hand on either side. She was playing an entry-level version of I Spy. 'I seeeeeeeee a bus!' she said, dragging out the see for dramatic impact. 'I seeeeeeeeee a tree!'

she said. 'I seeeeeeeeee a dog!' she said, stopping to point out each object along the way in that meandering way that small children have. 'I seeeeeeeeeeee Black people,' she said loudest of all, laughing. Her parents, mortified, cupped the child's mouth as if she had just yelled the word 'cunt' at the top of her lungs. And then the father turned around and apologised. She was talking about us.

12 LOSS

EBELE OKOBI

My son was the first born of twins. Twin A. When he was born, he weighed six pounds, nine ounces. Smallish for a single birth, but a healthy size for an early twin. He had an enormous head, beyond the ninety-ninth percentile, they told me, and in those early days, when everything about him was a complete mystery, a head 'bigger than the ninety-ninth percentile' felt like a win. He had the most insistent cry, and he ate incessantly, like he was in a hurry to grow up. Both of the twins had jaundice, so they slept under the glare of bilirubin lights until we were allowed to take them home. When they were five days old, we packed them up and went back to the hospital for a check-up. I handed the nurse my son, and she said, 'What large hands he has! I bet he'll be a great football player.'

I knew she meant well. And maybe it was something she said to all of the parents of baby boys. I couldn't quite trust my judgment in those early days of motherhood. I felt like I was swimming above ground, dazed and

131

druggy from getting one night's worth of sleep over five nights, and I was almost violently hyper-alert to potential threats. But I remember feeling, in that moment, that a story was already being written about my son. Big, in a country where stature is sufficient justification for murdering a Black man. And how did my tiny newborn have big hands, and if he did, could he not use those hands to be a surgeon, or a pianist?

And that's when I knew I did not have the courage, the heart, to raise a Black son in America.

America was built by Black people on a foundation of blood and bones, and appears to require a perpetual sacrifice of Black children to stay alive. For Black people, claiming America as home seems only possible in defiance. A bloody but unbowed 'I'm still here!!' Forever strangers in a strange land.

I knew then that I could not do what millions of Black parents do: send my child out, every day, into a country that would refuse to acknowledge his humanity. I felt that I could not survive knowing that my pride in him would always be mixed with terror. With every 'grown up' haircut. (Should he get a fade? But fades are threatening! Imagine having this conversation about a three-year-old child. Just imagine.) With every new clothing and shoe size, every new grade, having to ask: Is this the year he is old enough to be a threat?

So, in those first few days of my son's life, I decided to run. We moved to London in September of 2014, when my son was almost but not quite two years old.

We were expats, not immigrants. Money, a job, a relocation package and, above all, a choice made us 'not refugees'. In the beginning, when people would ask why we moved to London, I'd always have to decide whether to tell the real story ('I cannot raise Black children in America') or the socially acceptable version ('I got an amazing job!'). The closer the US election loomed, the easier it was to tell the truth. After Trump was elected I stopped worrying about making my exile easy for others and only ever told the truth.

There is enormous privilege in being able to choose where one belongs. The family my husband and I made came from Nigerian immigrants to the US on one side, descendants of stolen Africans and their captors on the other, and we were choosing to live in a country that is the root of the plunder on both sides. We chose London because most police do not carry guns, because there were less police killings in the UK in one year than there were in the state of California in one week. We would joke about how when white parents considered where to live, they thought about school achievement measures, number of parks, existence of local libraries, yoga studios. Black parents like us thought about all of those things, and also about all of the ways that the neighbourhood could punish our children for being Black.

My husband and I thought a lot about how we wanted to raise our children, how we wanted them to learn about and experience being Black. We wanted them to know that they are connected to a pan-African family.

We wanted them to feel that they would never be alone in the world. Most of all, we wanted being Black to represent joy. When they were babies, we were so careful about buying dolls with brown skin and tightly curled hair, about reading books with carefree Black children who weren't overcoming anything or being Symbols of Struggle. We thought that there was plenty of time to fill them up with love, before they found out that being Black could mean something other than joy.

Then after weeks of being curiously withdrawn and angry, my sweet three-year-old son told me that his London preschool teacher had called him a 'stupid little Black boy'. He only felt safe enough to whisper it to me after he had had such a bad day that I removed him from the school, only after he had asked 'Mommy, will I have to go back?' and I told him he'd never have to go back. I felt I had failed. Failed to prepare him, sure. (But how does one prepare a three-year-old for that? I had no idea.) Most of all, I felt I had failed because I had not anticipated the threat. I'd been watching for men with guns and forgotten about all of the other ways to hurt a Black child.

My solution, again, was to run. The next summer, we packed up the children and went to Ghana, then Senegal for the summer. I will never forget the joy on my son's face when we flew on a plane filled with brown people, stepped out of the airport into Accra's warm embrace, played on the beach in Dakar with another brown boy he called his best friend, after only having met him ten minutes before.

From that summer on, we promised the children that we would spend every summer surrounded by Black folk, by joy. The following summer we spent in Nigeria, and as soon as the children left the plane they pronounced themselves at home. When we flew from Lagos to Abuja, my then five-year-old son beamed when he was invited to the cockpit and met a Black pilot and crew, and shrieked with excitement when we landed at an airport with his name, Nnamdi. AN AIRPORT!! WITH HIS NAME!! One of their favourite activities was going to an indoor play attraction called Upbeat. Upbeat played nonstop Naija pop at top volume, was filled with screaming Black children literally bouncing off of the walls and was a guaranteed migraine for adults. I loved it, though, because it felt like the embodiment of Black boy and girl joy. I also loved it because I knew that the all Black staff would never single out my children, and my children alone, for being 'too aggressive'.

I couldn't be sure how many weeks of Davido and indoor trampolines and Dakar beaches cancelled out 'stupid little Black boy', but watching the children that summer in Nigeria, I felt I could unclench.

On 3 October of that year, I was in bed, pretending to be asleep. My son had woken early, as usual, and had climbed into bed. Nightmare, thirsty, needed an extra hug or a combination of the three. When I noticed my mother had called five or six times during the night, I called her back, and she was incoherent. When she could finally speak, she said, 'They killed him.' She told me that my youngest brother, Chinedu, had been tased to death by police in San Mateo County, California. For a second, I was the child and forgot I was a mother with children of my own to protect, and screamed, 'He's dead?' I can still picture my son's worried face, and how his question 'Mommy, who died?' snapped me back.

I still remember feeling, irrationally, terrified that my son being in the room when I found out meant something horrible. He kept asking who died, and I remember telling him that his uncle had died, in a car accident. What was I meant to say?

The morning was a blur of whispered phone calls, as I tried to pack, book plane tickets and keep from panicking in front of the children, who seemed to materialise in every corner in which I tried to hide. The flight was endless. Oceans of time to think about my brother.

Chinedu was born the day before Valentine's Day, so close to the brother before him that people used to think they were twins. He had irresistibly chubby cheeks when he was a baby, which was unfortunate because he clearly found the resulting cheek-pinching entirely beneath his dignity. He was the last of we five, and my memories of him all involve constant motion and extreme truth telling from a child who barrelled everywhere on extremely bowed legs. Once, when he was three years old, he solemnly informed our Sunday school teacher that he should chew some gum because he had bad breath. (He was not wrong, and feedback is a gift.)

When he graduated from Morehouse we were all so

proud — he was smart, funny, hard-working and incredibly kind, with an earnest streak that I found hilarious. He called me Little Big Sis, because he was six foot three and I am five foot four but still (always!) the bossy older sister.

He met a great girl, and they had a beautiful daughter, and I remember saying that I couldn't believe that the kid whose diapers I had changed was now changing diapers of his own.

While he was studying for the Graduate Management Admission Test, in his very early twenties, the voices started. We struggled for years to get him the right diagnosis and medications, and we were so proud of him for creating a good and kind life despite his struggles with mental health.

My brother was a kind, gentle person. He was loved by his family, yes, but he was also loved by his caseworkers, his managers at work, his friends. Even while struggling with mental illness, he brought people joy. That he would be killed by police was incomprehensible. It also felt entirely inevitable.

When I got home, the days were a horror of arrangements, the logistics of death. The very worst day, the day I've done my best to forget, was the day we went with my mother to see my brother's body. She screamed for what felt like decades, and I felt every wail in my bones. I experienced them as a child watching my mother being broken, and also as a fellow mother of a Black son, and it was the most unbearable thing to witness.

Police killings of Black people are so frequent in the

US that it seemed to me there should be a brochure, or a website, 'So Your Loved One Has Been Killed by the State', with step-by-step instructions, discounts, illustrations. There's the lawyer to be found, the activists to be engaged, the press to address.

In the first couple of days, my primary emotion was grief, but by the end of that long week, it had turned to rage, a focused commitment to make sure my brother's memory was a blessing, and a promise to him and my family to seek justice.

One of the most horrible things about police killings of Black people is how the victims are immediately stripped of their humanity, and convicted of their own deaths. So I wanted to make sure that we, and not his killers, told his story. I wrote a post on Facebook about my brother and about our family's loss. I spoke to Shaun King, the anti-racism activist, and he amplified my post. Overnight, my brother's death become a national and then an international story. I did dozens of interviews, and thousands of people responded, and reached out to me.

What was remarkable is how many people said, 'I thought this couldn't happen to you.' So many people told me that they had heard me say that I moved to London because I feared state violence and believed that raising children under its threat required parents to live in terror, to teach their children how to behave like enslaved people in order to escape it. They told me that they'd always thought I was being dramatic, exaggerating, illogical.

By 'you', they meant they thought it couldn't happen to educated people, middle-class people, people who went to boarding school and Ivy League law schools, or people with passports they used to travel to Europe, as opposed to shit-hole countries. They thought that privilege would protect people like me.

There was, and is, something uniquely horrible about that sentiment. I would hear it and realise that all of these centuries of Black people being brutalised by white supremacy, and white people still didn't understand how pervasive it is, how it warps the lives of every single Black person in America. I realised how much of our pain was discounted by good white people. But most of all, it became shockingly clear how little value was placed on Black lives. Because what people were really saying, what they meant, is that those 'other' people, those without privilege, somehow deserved to die. That in order for a Black life to begin to have value, it would need to be swaddled in privilege.

One of the most indelible moments of the nightmarish first week after my brother's death was when my mother, family and close friends were sitting in our lawyer's office for the first time. One of the many horrible circumstances of my brother's killing was that he had been taken to the hospital and no one had called us, no one had called his family. He'd lain for hours, alone, in the hospital, and then was transferred directly to the morgue, as if he had no one who loved him. I remember telling the lawyers this, saying that we needed answers, saying that this was wrong. As if this were the worst thing. I will never forget how the lawyer, who had been soothing and hyper-professional, turned to me and said, 'You know these white people don't care about you.'

I realised, in that moment, that the questions I was asking were predicated upon my belief that my brother's life mattered, that our family's grief mattered. Even after all I knew about how little value was placed on Black life, my reactions indicated my belief that we would be different.

Almost a year after my brother's death, I am learning more about grief, about solidarity, and even more about courage. It takes a special kind of courage to parent Black children, a specific kind of defiance. I've just read a book called *We Live for the We: The Political Power of Black Motherhood*. I loved this book, so much, because it reflects what feels most true to me, as a mother of Black children, especially in this moment in which we find ourselves. There is no safe space, privilege cannot protect any of them, and running doesn't work. According to the book, 'our obligation is to leave the world better for them and to ensure that they are equipped with the tools that they need to fight. We don't have the luxury of living normal lives. [. . .] We don't live for the I. We live for the we.'

Today my son is six years old. All the baby roundness has completely given way to sharp bones and muscle. He's obsessed with soccer and chess and riding his bike, and he's thrilled that his head (it's still enormous) reaches almost to my shoulders. But he still draws me pictures that say 'I love you Mommy', still asks me to carry him to bed, still wakes up with nightmares wanting a hug. We are still figuring out how to both protect and prepare him and his sisters for the world as it is, while equipping them to fight for the world as it should be. I still haven't told him how his uncle died.

One of the lines from *We Live for the We* will stay with me always: 'We are raising children who were never meant to survive.' I feel, so deeply, that raising brilliant, courageous Black children who will grow up to live lives in service while also feeling entitled to joy truly is revolutionary.

13 SO WE DON'T DIE TOMORROW

JESSICA HORN

Life, a friend of mine once declared, is a constant process of fighting against that which seeks to erase you from the world. It struck me as an exhausting idea. To be forced into a perpetual defence, ever ready to write yourself back in, or thrust your hand and stop your history from being obliterated before you have a chance to say '… that's just not true!' But I have found myself — as an African feminist and a Black woman working in the worlds of global human rights and development practice — repeatedly doing just that.

I was in my mid-teens when a wave of crisis hit the Great Lakes with the 100 days that marked the genocide in Rwanda. I always felt an intimacy with this history, given my mother's family's location in western Uganda, near enough to the borders of Rwanda and the Democratic Republic of Congo to be implicated in their legacies of displacement. A poem that I wrote as an undergraduate reflecting on the United Nations' use of wordplay to allow genocide to continue won first prize in a competition judged by my writing heroine, African American poet and essayist June Jordan. I felt 'seen', as we say on Black Twitter, felt an echo back from this accomplished observer of social beauty and political discord. During my master's degree I found myself revisiting this same terrain, spending several distressed weeks reading accounts of the language and metaphor used by genocidaires to describe the rape of Tutsi women.

I could never quite place a finger on what it was that drew me to the role of witness to brutality. I am not macabre in my tastes, and much prefer joyful experiments in creativity to engaging with the violence that punctuates so many women's lives. And yet I have constantly found myself in these spaces of bloody disagreement, metaphorical armour acting as a buffer for my permeable inner landscape, trying to stop the most horrific stories from entering and wreaking havoc. And so in June of 2012 there I was, coursing through verdant landscape in a Toyota Corolla. Soukous pulsing out of the windows as we swerved left and right on the winding road that led us away from Rwanda's capital Kigali and towards Lake Kivu and the small bridge that marked the border between Rwanda and its giant of a neighbour, the Democratic Republic of Congo.

I was on a trip with a small group of African feminist colleagues for a practical solidarity visit to Panzi Hospital in Bukavu, the capital of one of Congo's eastern provinces, and a central node in the armed conflict that had emerged from layers of regional historical grievances, lucrative mining interests, and the reality that business thrives in chaos. 'Women of the Congo' were in the process of becoming their own meme, a global salvation project, shorthand for the victimisation of African women's bodies, and the presumption that all violence against women in conflict is in the form of rape by rebel forces. American celebrities had already begun their descent, with public fundraisers and dance-offs in London and New York, and photoshoots with the brave women of this apparent epicentre of hell on earth. Panzi Hospital was at the core of this story — an increasingly visible experiment in activist medical care and survivor-centred medical response.

The air began to cool as we drove into the forested mountains. As I kept my motion sickness at bay I thought about what we were driving ourselves towards. By the wisdom of international media, Congo was a land of death. But I could also hear the tone of my mother's tongue rounding out the 'r' in the name 'Zaire'— as many East Africans of her generation still called it — the land of Lumumba. Birthplace of Congolese rumba. Of Franco and the TPOK Jazz tunes that I listened to on Sunday afternoons in my parents' house. This land of La Sape, of sartorial flamboyance.

It is easy to forget that life continues in the shadow of war. Small stalls selling vegetables and fruits lined the dusty roads of Bukavu's town centre, as people criss-crossed in traffic heading to work, or school, or market, or a friend's house. We passed a bakery called Peace and a mobile phone shop marketing itself with a painted portrait of a Blackberry-wielding Barack Obama. Our hotel was a quick trip from the border, and I settled into my room for the night. The next morning, we climbed into a Land Cruiser for the journey from town to Panzi Hospital. Once off the main road the car started to lurch as the stone-filled road challenged the heavy vehicle to a duel. I gripped the seat in front as we made our way down the hill in plumes of red dust until we reached the gates of the old mission hospital.

In comparison to the road outside, Panzi Hospital's grounds were immaculately swept. Low concrete buildings with wards formed the core of the medical complex, with shrubs dotting the edges of buildings. We were greeted and led to a grassy courtyard that formed the site for morning prayers. I was asked to address the staff, which I did in a mix of French and faltering Kiswahili, as our delegation was greeted in song, prayer and words of gratitude. By mid-morning we were on a tour of the compound. The line for the antenatal unit was long but orderly, as nurses in neat uniforms attended to pregnant mothers coming in for their monthly checks. We were shown the blood bank, the general wards, the HIV clinic. Though calm, the murmurs of war were not too far beneath the surface. We entered one of the waiting rooms to find a number of women sitting on the floor with their babies on their laps. The smell was strong, and the medic that was guiding us whispered quietly, 'It is the fistula — these women have survived rapes, and they are leaking urine.' Walking through the lab I spotted a sign pinned to a shelf that stated matter-of-factly: 'Travaillons comme si nous n'allons pas mourir demain'— Let's work as if we are not going to die tomorrow.

This mantra it seems has guided the work of Dr Denis Mukwege, medical director of Panzi Hospital, who had resuscitated the old hospital in the midst of conflict, building it into a centre of medical innovation on gynaecological surgery and holistic, justice-fuelled response to violence against women. Work that would win him a Nobel Peace Prize. A baobab tree of a man, Mukwege's frame filled the door of his office as he walked out to greet us. His white medical coat and rubber clogs signalled his profession, just as the over-curved bend in his shoulders signalled his calling as mender of women's pain. That evening we were invited to his house for dinner, and we sat around his family table as he and his wife offered nourishment with the generosity of old friends. Dr Mukwege and I ended up talking into the evening. I shared that my grandfather came from the mountains on the Congo-Uganda border, summoning in me a sense of historical responsibility to this region. He shared his life story and what had compelled him to do this work, choosing to return to Congo rather than remain in the West and a relatively easy life of private medical practice. His vision had clearly inspired a dedicated staff base, faced as they were with ongoing challenges to their own physical security and mental health. I saw, in the outreach projects Panzi had established to support its women patients, that this wilful commitment to thrive in defiance of human cruelty was shared. Women patients who had been handed the repercussions of armed grievances that were not theirs — lost families, fractured physical bodies, disrupted livelihoods — working together in a resilient solidarity to make their worlds anew. In the simplest of words, what I saw of Panzi's work was remarkable. As our car left Bukavu I was overcome with a sense of triumph.

On the flight back to London I struck up a conversation with the white woman sitting next to me. She was middle-aged, and from her accent clearly from a British upper-class background, by education at least if not by family position. She explained that she was working as a peace building consultant in Congo, but had recently started a business venture there. She asked what I was doing in Bukavu and I described the visit to Panzi Hospital. 'Mukwege,' she said. 'Well, his hospital is not as great as everyone says it is.' She proceeded with a decidedly salty analysis not just of Panzi Hospital but of what she felt was the fault of Congolese people for bringing war, and its horrors, upon themselves. I sensed almost a jealousy in her posture, as she launched critique after critique against the people of the country that was the source of her apparently buoyant livelihood.

I looked dead into her eyes and said, 'Well, I think that you and I have completely different understandings of history.' I proceeded with a quickfire analysis of the history of Congo, from its status as the personal property of King Leopold of Belgium, through the hope that Patrice Lumumba provided for political autonomy, to his slaughter at the hands of Western-backed assassins. That the Congo's mineral wealth had always been extracted to fuel northern militarism — even the uranium for the first atomic bombs dropped by the USA in Hiroshima and Nagasaki came from the soil of Congo. Her arrogance did not falter and she muttered back 'That is old news', and turned away, ending our conversation.

Anger can be clarifying. As the fire of fury rose in me, I realised how deeply African possibility is held hostage by 'experts' like this woman, who did not return the welcome offered by African communities by holding their future anywhere in her heart. To her the devastation of life in eastern Congo was a career opportunity, a business opportunity, a means to an end. Raw material for personal progression. I am not sure why I had expected her to be moved by my attempts at re-scripting her narrative. There was no real or imagined bloodline connecting her to the arteries of Bukavu's people. The truths of this land were, well, erasable. Her finger was casually positioned on delete.

In October of that year gunmen entered Dr Mukwege's home, pointed weapons at his two daughters and waited for him. As his car pulled in they managed to get as close as putting a gun to his head, before his watchman Joseph Bizmana intervened, sacrificing his own life instead. The news spread fast. Mukwege's own staff, friends and patients arrived first to stand guard. A group of women from Panzi's outreach projects even journeyed on foot from their homes on the outskirts of Bukavu, kitenge-clad sentinels coming to protect the beloved doctor. Mukwege was at risk. In recent speeches he had been writing the political economy of the conflict swirling around him back in to public record. Western mining companies, national political elites, the economy booming around eastern Congo's precarity, all forces that depended on an ever-dwindling memory of their presence to flourish.

Back in London, I chose the few solidarity tools at my disposal — an email to Dr Mukwege, text messages to colleagues to see how to stoke a political response — and my voice. In an article co-written with a colleague for *openDemocracy* we retraced the political underpinnings of the need for solidarity with Mukwege. To write against the emptying, the elision.

If activism is the affirmation of life, then perhaps it really is a battle against the backstory being erased from the world. Situated in history as woman, as feminist, African, Black, the path towards persistent presence is lit incandescent. To survive is to name troublesome truths. Loudly, at precarious moments.

In the midst of threat.

14 THE LORD'S HOUSE, A QUEEN'S SOUL

Whether you're religious, agnostic or atheist, it requires a certain amount of faith to carve out a place for yourself where there is none. To look at what one might consider a grim prospect and see the opposite: an opportunity to fly. And as Black women, that is what we do, and have done, for generations.

But what that faith looks like and where it comes from is changing for many of us. Historically, we have been more religious than most. (That's especially so in America where Black women make up 83 per cent of those who claim to be highly religious.) Scroll through our biggest changemakers, old and new — Fannie Lou Hamer, Angela Davis, Assata Shakur, Shirley Chisolm, Kimberlé Williams Crenshaw, Oprah Winfrey, Ava DuVernay, Tarana Burke, the list goes on. Powering most of them, if not all: an unwavering sense of self and purpose that seems deeply spiritual. And in more recent times, spirituality increasingly looks different for many of us. Less patriarchal, more female-centered. Less churchy, more witchy. Fewer pastel-coloured, wide-brimmed hats, more head wraps. Fewer Bibles, more bundles of sage.

The problem was that the church, in the historic sense, became sticky, repressive and, at times, oppressive. It represented all the ills: too homophobic, too sexist, and in the case of the historically white churches, too racist. So many women, including myself, simply stopped going. And that's even as our sense of purpose and need for some kind of spiritual grounding increased in this unusually unpredictable new decade. The church's complicated relationship with women is largely to blame.

For me this divide between our religious past and present, our transition from one kind of faith to another, became clear during an afternoon spent watching Aretha Franklin's funeral while getting my hair done in Notting Hill. The service highlighted just how much the church can alienate women and reminded me of the experiences in my own life that led me to walk away.

'Somebody swaddle Stevie Wonder in bubble wrap. He's all we got left,' a woman said as a stylist braided her hair. She was quoting a popular meme that would circulate whenever anyone of a certain generation of Black icons died. And there had been a string of these deaths in the space of just eight years, each one signalling not only the passage of time, but the end of an era. Michael Jackson — as controversial as he was (29 August 1958 – 25 June 2009). Whitney Houston (9 August 1963 – 11 February 2012). Prince (7 June 1958 – 21 April 2016). All deaths that rattled the collective consciousness, sending us into a state of mourning for our childhoods, carefree teen years, first loves, and the many other chapters of our lives their music stoked. All departures that heightened the feeling that nothing was solid and stable any more.

The making of a true icon is in the longevity, and the artist's ability to connect with another's soul at multiple touchpoints throughout time. And in so doing, the icon becomes something greater than musician. Something greater than the mere body. The icon borders on the spiritual. Aretha Franklin went two steps further. She was the daughter of a Black American minister and civil rights activist who became a towering figure in both the church and civil rights movement in her own right. Her music soundtracked many eras, yes, but she also connected the cultural, the political, the personal, and the religious.

So when the singer, songwriter, pianist and activist died on 16 August 2018 at 76 years old of pancreatic cancer, the world grieved. And I felt, for a moment, unmoored. But as I watched the funeral unfold over a slow-moving, eight-hour marathon, I gained clarity on why I had to let my attachments to the evangelical religion of my formative years go, and release the identity it had imposed on me. It was only in finding a new faith that I was able to grow into a fuller version of myself.

To be frank, I had never given Aretha Franklin much thought until I reached adulthood. I don't recall my parents playing her music as I was growing up. Aretha didn't factor in among the Stevie Wonder, Luther Vandross and

Earth, Wind and Fire albums in their music library. And yet she was always around, her music seeping into every crevice of our life, seasoning it like a boullion cube, its flavour transforming everything it touched. I heard Aretha's music on the radio, at church and on television. But her anthems also inspired the music that filled my childhood home: Whitney Houston, Chaka Khan and Mariah Carey.

In many ways, she was the soundtrack to my life, even if I hadn't particularly noticed it. Before I knew what feminism was or how to cite theory, I knew the words to 'Respect'. And her cover of 'Young, Gifted and Black' underscored my earliest lessons in Black pride long before I learned the language to articulate it.

Her influence spread far and wide, like any queen's would, stretching across generations, continents and countries, all the way over here to the UK.

And like a true queen, Aretha's passing demanded extended days of viewings and mourning, commanding the kind of media coverage that rivalled the deaths of some of history's more popular heads of state, starting with a public viewing on a Tuesday and ending on a Saturday night after a particularly long funeral, which included an impressive line-up of outfit changes (because, queen) in between.

The world was riveted from the word go: an image of Aretha in glamorous, peaceful repose inside a gold-plated Promethean casket, enveloped in overflowing pink and lavender roses, her ankles delicately crossed to reveal red, sky-high custom Christian Louboutin stilettos on her feet.

The red shoes, which matched her red chiffon and lace dress, lips and nails, were meant to signify her membership in the historically Black sorority Delta Sigma Theta. Outside the Charles H. Wright Museum of African American History, once the largest Black museum in the country, where the viewing was taking place, a pink Cadillac, the same one that was used to carry Rosa Parks' body to her funeral decades ago, stood at attention.

Over the following days, there would be more outfit changes, in pale robin's egg blue and rose gold, and more Louboutins — clothes befitting a woman one mourner described to the Associated Press as 'a diva to the end'.

The funeral was naturally momentous. So there we were, at 2.30 p.m. in Charlotte Mensah's salon in Notting Hill, clients and hairstylists tuning in to a marathon of mourning in honour of an icon and a woman of faith. Meanwhile, Black Twitter was live Tweeting, #ArethaHomegoing commentary unfolding in real time with the velocity usually reserved for the Oscars and Grammys. And no wonder: the programme was ambitious, as most Black church gatherings are, with fifty-two scheduled special guests, performers, pastors and choirs slated to sing, sermonise and pray. Aretha, icon that she was, deserved it.

What she didn't deserve from the epic memorial was the sexism, as a string of senior-ranking preachers and bishops' acts of misogyny not only stole the show, but displayed the Black church's fraught history with women to all.

I was at the salon to get my hair braided, an experience that, like church, can be incredibly time-consuming, though rewarding. I wondered which would take longer: the homegoing or the hair-braiding. The stylist assured me the braiding would be shorter. I explained that where I come from, deep in America's Bible Belt, the Black church services aren't a sprint, but a marathon of prayer, praise dance, offering, sermon, alter call, Baptism and communion (because the blood of Jesus can't be rushed) — all that worship ending with a lunch consumed so late in the afternoon it was commonly called a church dinner.

The stylist explained that it was the same in Ghana, where two thirds of the population is Christian and prayer services can run all night.

We watched Bill and Hillary Clinton greet Jesse Jackson and Tyler Perry. And Jennifer Hudson walk in with security guards. And Ariana Grande whisper into boyfriend Pete Davidson's ear before all taking their seats. We watched a choir that looked to be seven rows deep sing the gospel anthem, 'I Shall Wear A Crown', as Bill Clinton and Jesse Jackson stood up again, and a processional of clergy and family members stretching the entire length of the stadium, worked their way down the aisle to the casket. We watched children, and grandchildren, and cousins, and childhood friends, and church brothers and sisters, one by one, pay their respects before heading to their seats as the choir's voices rose an octave ('I'll hasten to his throne') and the congregation's hands began to wave and pump in the air with emotion.

In the background, a woman's voice wailed, 'Oh God help me', as relatives lowered the lid, closing the casket. On stage, Shirley Caesar wiped away tears.

We were 3,748 miles away and the emotion was palpable. Aretha's homegoing was already running nearly two hours late, before it had even really begun. All of us in the salon, our childhoods spanning multiple African, North American and European countries, recognised it for what it really was: church, in all its flawed glory.

Compared to my parents' and their parents' day, the Black American church — a shorthand that, depending on where you grew up, could mean any one of the following: National Baptist Convention of America, Progressive National Convention, Christian Methodist Episcopal Church, National Baptist Convention, Church of God in Christ, African Methodist Episcopal Church or the African Methodist Episcopal Zion Church — had been on a downswing. Over the past decade, membership had been on a steep decline, as millennials and Xers went the way of New Age, with its mindfulness and healing crystals, or gravitated toward the very religions we were warned against — the traditional African ones — embracing Yoruba, Hoodoo, Voodoo, Ifa, and Santería to name a few.

Neither the Black nor the white Christian church has been exempt from all the conversation around inclusivity. Perhaps this is why, in 2018, the Church of England launched a diversity initiative encouraging Black, brown and LGBTQ+ people to become vicars. And in 2019 it finally appointed its first ever Black female bishop, Rose Hudson-Wilkin. Jamaican-born and a child of the Windrush generation, she had spent years calling the church out for its entrenched institutionalised racism. She told BBC News, 'It's really a heavy burden to say that because that is the Church that I belong to, that is the Church that I love, but if someone else can genuinely give me another rationale as to why we are not there in senior leadership roles within the Church, then I'm prepared to consider it.' When Rose recognised her 'calling' to become a woman of faith, there were very few women bishops. In an interview with *Vogue*, she explained, 'For me, the vocation was about leadership, pastorally caring for people and guiding in the liturgy. It was quite strange, given that no women were allowed to occupy such roles then, to feel called to something that didn't exist.'

The Church of England is almost half a millennium old. Maybe it's too little too late. Many of the women I know on both sides of the Atlantic stopped going to church of any denomination long ago.

By that same token, while my religious literacy as a teen was rooted in Sunday Bible school and weekly choir rehearsals, as an adult it has been informed by experiences as vast as meditating in a sixteenth-century Buddhist temple in Japan, to shopping for candles in a Puerto Rican botanica in East Harlem. It's a mixed bag. Many of my girlfriends have grown into the exact kind of women their parents told them to steer clear of: atheists, witches, believers in Voodoo and practitioners of root work. Some lighting candles and casting spells, all setting intentions. And they are hardly a minority. Black witchy behaviour has infiltrated pop culture from Beyoncé's *Lemonade*, rich in Yoruba imagery and references, to Princess Nokia's hit, 'Bruja's'. Literal, actual Black Girl Magic.

Aretha's funeral made it clear to me how we got here, swerving organised religious institutions that continuously sidelined us in favour of theologies, both old and New Age, that allowed Black women to step into our power.

My own faith is the sum of many parts, informed by the full spectrum of Christian and folk traditions I've encountered in my life. And my soul is all the richer — and sense of who I am and who I am not, all the clearer — because of it.

My own church attendance dropped off in my early twenties after a stint in a mega-church in New York and a childhood spent between the two poles of Black church-going in Virginia: in one corner, the tiny wooden chapel my grandmother occasionally took me to, made up of one room about the size of a corner store, with hard wooden pews and burgundy leather-bound bibles. Its small congregation was filled with white-gloved grandmothers like mine, women who favoured pastel-coloured dresses, patent leather purses and pert hats. In the other corner: the sleek, sprawling Southern Baptist church I attended with my mom. It was plush and ever-growing thanks to an especially robust new building fund raised by its congregation of upwardly mobile worshipers. There was a bustling Sunday school, a newly opened wing with an overflow room and crisp offices for the clergy. Its choir was a fixture in gospel competitions and the pastor regularly hosted visits by high-profile ministers from other cities. The church was on the map.

Despite the latter being my church home, I felt no more connected to it than my grandmother's. As much as I loved the sense of history and community, I felt detached and isolated from the group. Even if I looked the part, with my pressed and curled hair, frilled dress and patent leather shoes, I didn't feel wholly at home with the idea of Black girlhood I was expected to embody there. I didn't see myself in the idea of Southern Black womanhood I was expected to grow into. There was nothing wrong with it. It just didn't feel me. Surrounded by a children's ministry full of popular little deacons and deaconesses in the making, many of whom were debutantes and members of Black middle-class youth clubs like Jack and Jill, there seemed to be no room for my isms and quirks — my social awkwardness, my love of secular music, my fascination with whales, my obsession with Bill T. Jones, Baryshnikov and Bob Fosse, my overall discomfort with talking to, let alone hugging, strangers...

And most of all, I struggled with the politics even when I didn't have the vocabulary to pinpoint why I was uneasy. Instinctively, I would squirm when sermons would turn towards subjects like the role of a woman, wife and mother in the home or the perils of homosexuality.

Even then, the church felt paradoxical in its insistence on being male-centred. Because what was the Black church without the Black women who constituted more than seventy per cent of its membership? I was surrounded by dynamic matriarchs, women who as my grandmother would say, 'ruled the roost'. And yet within the context of the church, an institution known for advancing the rights of Black people as a whole, women were largely unequal and relegated to the roles of usher, secretary and children's ministry — confined to the sidelines, despite disproportionately filling up the pews.

During my time at college, the disillusionment slowly increased when I joined an international church, which appeared more progressive and modern, with a congregation that originated from various countries across the world. And yet, I began to question its stance on sex and abortion. Despite my increasing misgivings, I remained a member, going on to attend a north-east branch after I graduated school and moved to New York. The congregation, filled with charismatic working models, designers, actors and playwrights, of all ethnicities and backgrounds, seemed geared towards young aspiring creatives like me and felt like a safe space in a big city of hustlers. But increasingly, I began to feel like I was the one being hustled and lied to. The church became an echo chamber of oppressive values, teaching that dating and any other kind of relationship-building should take place within the church. Men dominated the leadership and their teachings began to feel against my best interests, even if their sermons and lectures were delivered with a mock self-deprecation ('I might be the one standing on stage, but we all know my wife really runs the show'). Things began to feel sinister when a women's ministry leader gave a sermon on marriage and spoke with great passion about why wives must prioritise their husband's sexual demands above their own. As my own feminist awakening grew, it became clear to me that this was not an empowering place for women. My church attendance dropped off completely at that point.

Some friends and family members argued I had simply gone to the wrong churches. But my mind was made up and I didn't think much more about it — until 2017 when the church had had a few high-profile moments, thanks to Meghan's wedding to Prince Harry, in which a Black preacher from Chicago and a gospel choir turned Windsor Castle into a Southern American chapel with rousing songs and a sermon.

Aretha Franklin's funeral felt similarly significant, projecting the rituals of the 11 a.m. service onto screens around the world, including the one we sat around here in London, where more than half the city's residents claim to have no religion.

I felt homesick, like a child longing for the familiarity of a dysfunctional family.

'Is she dressed for a funeral or the club?' a client asked, ninety minutes into the programme, as we watched Ariana Grande do her final vocal runs while singing 'Natural Woman'. In the audience, there were no shoulders shaking with emotion, no heads swaying and hanging low — signals of any good gospel performance. Instead, there was restrained, polite applause.

'It's disrespectful, that dress. Too short,' she added.

But I was more distracted by Bishop Charles Ellis III who had just made a joke about Ariana's name sounding like a Taco Bell meal and was now clutching her at the waist, his fingers grazing her breast. A quick check of Twitter confirmed I wasn't seeing things. People were scandalised. But not all of them were angry about the same thing I was. There were those outraged at the sight of Ariana being manhandled. And others irritated by Ariana's audacity to attend 'the FUNERAL FOR THE QUEEN', to quote one Tweet, in 'the house of the Lord', to quote another, wearing a little skimpy dress.

The funeral was in fact taking place in a museum. But the building was irrelevant.

When Aretha went into a studio on Valentine's Day in 1967 and recorded 'Respect', the word meant something different entirely. Otis Redding originally wrote it as a love song that reinforced a certain kind of storyline. He worked hard for his money, which he in turn gave to his woman. The least she could do was respect him when he got home.

But Aretha's version reoriented the conversation. The person doing the demanding had changed. She was a woman. A Black woman. A Black woman rooted in the Black church. And a Black woman, demanding respect and human dignity, during a time when Black pride was on the rise and women were rebelling against the patriarchy, much as we are now.

We now live in an age in which there are few new ideas, only new ways of presenting them. But when Aretha sang 'Respect', the song was revolutionary. The world wasn't used to seeing a Black woman hold it to account.

She had taken the hallmarks of church music — the volcanic holler, righteous indignation, soulful call-and-response and stomach-stirring rhythm — and flipped it inside out, rendering the old gendered power structure null and void.

Surely, the image of a pastor clutching at a pop star like a hot burrito undermined Aretha's entire legacy. 'Aretha must be rolling over in her casket,' I said. 'Mmmmmmmhmmmmm,' the woman sat next to me in the salon agreed.

'Aretha was a Black woman in a white man's world,' Al Sharpton eulogised, an hour later. The week had been filled with extended obituaries and think pieces, all contributing to a pre-digested narrative of Aretha as church-going, purse-holding, feminist and civil rights icon. But I had yet to hear anyone sum her life up as such: a woman navigating a world of difference during a time when many viewed dissimilarity as a crippling handicap rather than the currency it is now.

Her music amplified Black pride and creativity during a Black renaissance. We're seeing a similar renaissance now, except, unlike then, feminism and civil rights are no longer bad for business.

In her essay, 'Dear Black Man', the writer Fran Sanders describes the Black woman as the one who for 'two hundred years initiated the dialogue between the white world and the Black.' Aretha was a daughter of this legacy. As are we.

'I think that's enough church now.' The shampoo girl had turned the funeral off and replaced the gospel songs with a playlist of house music.

But I was still hooked and had tuned in to the funeral via my phone, watching it through to the end of my appointment and car ride home. By the time I reached my sofa, with a carton full of Chinese takeaway in hand, Chaka Khan was singing 'Going Up Yonder'. The last time I had heard the song was as a child, singing in the youth choir during my home church's revival. We were three songs into our programme, having successfully performed the set list we rehearsed every Tuesday night after school, when moved by the emotion of a praise break, our choir director changed tack and began singing an intro I had never heard before.

'If you want to know
Where I'm going, soon'

Without missing a beat, the kids around me picked up the chorus: 'I'm going up yooooooonder.' I was mortified; had I missed a rehearsal? I knew I hadn't. When and where had they all learned this song? Unlike some families, mine didn't spend every evening at a church activity (nor did we even spend every Sunday in service, for that matter). But I rarely missed a rehearsal in the run-up to revival, my favourite moment on the worship calendar, mostly because it involved twice as much of what I considered to be the best parts of church: gospel music and good food. Had I missed an impromptu practice?

So I stood there and tried to mouth the words as best I could, lest I give away the fact that I was caught unprepared. And eventually, my embarrassment gave way to emotion, as the blend of bass, baritone, alto and soprano settled into a sweet vocal mille-feuille. By the time the second chorus rolled around, I had gotten the hang of the words. 'Going up yooooondeeeerr.'

By the time the song ended I had gone from feeling like an outsider to a member of Jesus' inner circle.

But watching the funeral, a Reverend now controversially declaring that a 'Black woman cannot raise a Black boy to be a man', I felt more like a prodigal daughter, a crystal-carrying child of the Baptist church, refusing to go home. We were all tired by that point, when the Reverend Jasper Williams began his eulogy by taking a shot at the woman he was there to celebrate, a single mother of four boys. More criticism of Aretha followed: 'Black lives must not matter until Black people start respecting Black lives and stop killing ourselves.' Twitter recoiled at the man's archaic rebuke, which ended more than thirty minutes later with an altar call. 'The only thing Black America needs today more than anything else, is to come back home to God… A home is what I see Black people need more than a house.'

Or maybe it was time for Black women to dismantle that house — a house in which their voices were diminished and a man had been allowed to have the last word on the legacy of a queen — and build a new one.

It seemed odd for a woman famous for answering to no one but God, to be eulogised by not only a man, but one with such archaic views in a programme so light on women speakers. In theory, religion is that thing that helps one make sense of the world. But coming from the mouth of Jasper Williams, religion sounded like one of the biggest problems in the world, a danger to women. Less the conduit to freedom, more the shackles around her feet.

'We can talk about all the things that are wrong, and there are many. But the only thing that can deliver us is love.' Tub of ice cream in hand now, I was committed to seeing the marathon through to the end, detours and all. Stevie Wonder, the final act on the programme, God bless him, had managed to reorient the focus back to the queen, while rebuking Williams at the same time. 'Because Black lives do matter, because all lives do matter and if we love God then we know truly that it is our love that will make all things matter, when we make love great again. That is what Aretha has said throughout her life. Throughout the pain, she gave us the joy and said, "Let's make love great again."'

I watched my feed fill up with approving 'tape Stevie up in bubble wrap' posts. But the sentiment that he's all we have left felt flippant and wrong. Eight hours later, my cup, to borrow the language of Biblical analogy, felt empty. From a hair salon in west London, through a cab ride home, dinner and bed, I clutched my screen looking for memories of home and the seeds of purpose, promise and optimism I found during my earliest memories of church there. But the longer I watched, the more I was reminded of all the reasons I left religion as I knew it in America — even as my own feelings of purpose, and belief in something bigger than me, have intensified in adulthood and expatriation far, far away from any pastor's pulpit.

And as I turned the television off, I felt like I had witnessed the burial of much more than a queen. And I hoped that like the diva she was, those eight hours of mourning and the controversy they unleashed would lead to a longer-lasting upending, one that turns the world of organised religion into a place that deepens Black women's power rather than merely leaning on it.

15 INFERNO

I could see the smoke before I smelled it. It was around seven a.m. on a warm summer morning in June 2017. Traffic was a long, drawn-out snarl from Heathrow, winding its way down the M4 towards London at a lethargic pace. I had just returned from a work trip to Basel, dipping into the art and fashion bubble where I spent days perusing paintings and sculptures I could not afford and enjoying good food in the balmy Swiss sun. The cab driver and I listened to a BBC broadcaster bring the morning commuters up to speed: at least six people had died in a fire that engulfed a twenty-four-storey council block of 127 flats during the night. Witnesses could hear people screaming, pleading for help. The children. Other witnesses saw flashing lights, what appeared to be phones, blinking and waving in windows. There was a survivor. Thank God he hadn't listened to the official advice to stay inside his flat and instead grabbed his girlfriend and baby and ran like hell. It was Ramadan, some people were breaking fast. Others returning from prayers. At least seven hundred people were in the building, many of them sleeping when it started. We listened to a senior-ranking police officer describe the rescue as 'complex and lengthy'. So many people. How could they know how many people were in the building? I leaned forward so the driver could see my finger pointing between the two front seats towards a black cloud in the distance. 'Is that it down there?' I asked. 'I think so,' he said, shaking his head as we listened to the broadcaster explain that the building had just undergone renovations that one resident had complained presented a fire risk. Inquiries were being demanded from all sides. I calmed my abdomen, which was slightly swollen with nine weeks of growing pregnancy that would come to an end weeks later, and listened to the growing anger. So many people ignored. How would they ever know how many people had been killed? Surely, this would not have happened if they were rich. Or white. Like the residents of the multi-million pound houses that surrounded the largely poor, working-class Lancaster West Estate? So many people inside. Many Muslim, many from African countries. Immigrants. All of this in England's wealthiest borough. Who let this happen? Everyone. The class implications. The racial ones. The driver and I discussed them all.

It had been a horrible summer, which was the apex in a build-up of outrage. Just two weeks before, three men drove a van into crowds of people at London Bridge and then proceeded to stab and kill innocent bystanders at Borough Market. Weeks before that, a bombing at an

Ariana Grande concert in Manchester. Two months before that, a terrorist attack at Westminster Bridge.

And in the distance a tower block burned, angry like the year that wouldn't stop raging. A rising cloud of remnants cutting the air.

16 ON HAIR

FREDDIE HARREL

I like to believe we have a say in how we show up in every lifetime. I imagine each return to earth offers a different perspective and an opportunity for a new take on the bigger lesson we keep coming back to explore. For me, each return is tied to my hair.

There is no randomness to me being the woman I am or the Blackness wrapping her. The Black woman I am embodies a fierce commitment to defying the odds society stacks up against us, trying to slow us all down in the process.

For many of us, the bumps on the road appear early through messages — whether in in our schools and communities or in the magazines we read and television shows we watch — that our very nature isn't the blossoming kind. If it's not our faces and bodies that are wrong, we're being told it's our attitude, our mind. And as we grow, the messages threaten to seep deeper into the consciousness, even though intellectually we know they don't make sense. And yet there we are questioning ourselves and our sanity. Many of us internalise the false assumptions of who we are, and then in adulthood, have to learn how to undo the damage.

Growing up in the northern suburbs of Paris in my Cameroonian family, I never thought much about my hair or its texture. I can remember moments: staring at the way my ringlets would form round, bouncy, spring-like bursts after my mother washed my hair when I was in primary school. I remember the detangling that would happen afterwards, so painful it felt like my hair was fighting the comb. Then came the fragrant oils and creams. Then my cousins would style it with crimped braiding, my favourite. After all of this, my hair would smell delicious and remind me of summer.

Braiding is a time commitment. But when it's between mother and daughter, sisters, cousins or friends, it's also an act of love — one's hands passing through another's hair, the other's head lying in the braider's lap. That's why I believe sisterhood is drilled so deep into our DNA.

When I think of those early memories of getting my hair braided, I can also remember the prints on *maman*'s and *tata*'s dresses. The cowries we wore in our hair. The careful intricacies of the twists or the height of a pony-tail. I didn't get to wear my hair out or 'down', as we'd describe it back then. We didn't get to be carefree, hair blowing in the wind. But that's what made us, *us*. Our hair was beautiful. Every month I got to have a say in a new design and I'd plan which outfits or shoes I'd wear to complement the look.

As I grew older, my relationship with my hair became more complicated. When I was a small girl, I had a friend you'd always find me with on the weekends. Mélissa, my neighbour, who was Black, too, but West Indian. Her mother would put three twists in her hair, one at the front that would come down the side of her head, and two at the back, all three with big round pearls dangling and clinking at their ends.

I wanted in, mainly because her three ponytails looked like they took far less time to do than my braided ringlets. But when I convinced my sister to replicate the style on me, the results were disappointingly different. My three twists were tiny, hers were puffy and swirly.

Mélissa, explained the style didn't work on me because we had different hair textures. Hers, she said, came from her Indian ancestors. This is my first memory of what some would call 'good hair', an idea we all now know does more harm than good. And for a range of reasons, I'd see more of this kind of hair on African-American singers and actresses — their films, music videos and television shows opening my eyes to a new world that looked different to my own.

Eventually, my parents enrolled me in a Catholic private school, where I went from being one student in a melting pot of many ethnicities to one spot of colour in a sea of white. As one of fewer than ten Black students in a student body of roughly six hundred, I felt like my appearance was at odds with the natural order of things. Still, I knew my hair was this magical thing.

There were only a handful of us Black girls and we kept showing up to school each month with new beginnings on our heads — that's how each new style always felt to me.

Things took a turn when I hit the age of 14, when my cousins began to call me white because of the way I spoke or because my body was a skinny, hapless bag of bones they said no Black man in his right mind would ever settle for. So I started trying to prove my Blackness and in the process felt like I was failing at the very thing that was the most obvious about me. Meanwhile, at school I was too Black, where everything from my body to my very being was up for constant scrutiny. My small curves looked large in comparison to my white classmates. They'd call me *grosses fesses* ('big bum' in French). This was confusing to me.

One day my English Literature teacher even went as far as to call me out in front of the class, telling me my people have an arched back, as she traced a line with her finger down the dip in my spine to where it swerved into a pair of round butt cheeks, which she said were distracting the boys. She urged me to wear baggier clothes. I wanted out of this state of limbo, in which I felt too big and too small, too Black and not Black enough.

America, or at least the idea of it, seemed to offer a gateway. I discovered this at the age of 13 when a cousin, having returned from a visit to the States, gave me a present she bought during her travels there. 'Just For Me', the brand name in bright, graphic, multi-coloured type read on the box of hair relaxer. On its front, a photo of a little

Black American girl with smooth skin and long, straight, lustrous hair that curled at the ends. I was mesmerised. Perms were the latest African-American fashion to make its way over to France. The girl on the box was my first view of a global family that existed elsewhere. I'd imagine a world of Black people abroad, and in my future.

As for my hair, I got it relaxed. And my sister, who is seven years older than me, relaxed hers too. We'd curl our hair in rollers and, along with our cousins, give each other oil treatments every weekend. Relaxed hair is more fragile and prone to damage than it is in its natural state, but we were all figuring it out together. As we do.

I spent my teen years in the early aughts experimenting with a range of hairstyles, inspired by pop star versions of the little girl on the box. There was Aaliyah's long layers and Alicia Keys' braided crowns. At school I became popular for braiding my classmates' hair, replicating Alicia's zigzags. And my Blackness became a form of social currency.

This was also around the time when I discovered India. Arie and spent my weekends trying to translate her lyrics into French. I felt like, she GOT me. She looked happy and free, a place where I wanted to be. And then there was Jill Scott, who showed a strength I aspired to have. But none of my friends knew these singers. They were my secret happy place — a kind of contraband source of Black wisdom and inspiration.

A few years later, I went to business school, where I felt even more alien than I did at private school. I wasn't just

Black, but from the suburbs. Regardless, I did the braids, the roller sets, the experiments, and wore all the things that made me, me.

When I began a career in banking in Paris's financial district, I started experimenting with sew-in weaves. In a lot of my social circles, they were a visual signifier that you're doing okay in the world, polished and glamorous. So I followed suit. Not to mention having a weave could save time during the work week; I didn't need to spend extra minutes and hours doing my hair.

Most of all, I loved going to the salon to get the hair put in. It was another world. I loved sitting next to so many different kinds of women where everyone felt like family and we could be our lively selves, with a feeling of warmth on tap. With all the sew-ins, I stopped bothering with the hair relaxers. And as my original hair texture — those springy, bouncy ringlets — grew back in, it became crystal clear: this hair is precious.

I began to play with the texture, apart from the sew-ins. I wore an Afro and discovered a new face. My bone structure, exposed in a different light, took on a new shape: the big cheeks, the high cheekbones, the wide nostrils I never quite liked, the lips I was always unsure of, they all made sense now. I fell in love with my face, which was framed in the candy floss-like texture that grew out of my head — fuzz, jazz as I like to call it, moisturised in coconut oil. I fell in love with me all over again. And my facial features combined to tell a glorious tale. The change unleashed a more fully realised me, I leaned in to my personal style.

I'm a natural chatterbox, who likes to lay it all out. So when I discovered social media in the early 2010s, I began to find my space. I shared my hopes, struggles and wins online, but also documented the looks that helped me to express all those things. After having spent so long of my life feeling like a misfit, I found solace in being able to speak freely. It felt so natural, I barely noticed when my following grew from a few hundred to more than 230,000 — many of them Black, many of them learning to embrace the fullness of themselves like me.

In the span of a few years, the very attributes that alienated me when I was younger made me popular. And eventually, the Internet inspired me to launch a beauty startup that would allow women to buy and wear the very springy, bouncy coils (my life always coming back to the hair) that I loved so much growing up.

Hair has been a pivotal part of each life transition, from school to my years in banking and through to careers in fashion and now the world of beauty. I've survived toxic boyfriends and moves to new cities and countries (Paris, Hong Kong, London, Geneva, London again, and counting). I'm now an entrepreneur and business owner. A mother and a wife. And I now live in America, getting to know a new experience of Blackness, one that always makes me think of the child I was, staring at the little girl on the box.

Throughout my experiences living in all these places I've learned that the established history lessons of record that we're taught in our various birthplaces have told us far too little about each other among the diaspora. My time moving from one hair style to the next, from my cousin's lap to salons all over the world, have showed me the importance in letting the stories of ourselves out, showing each other the power in all our many shades and nuances.

I, for one, feel like I've lived a thousand lives wrapped into one and my hair is how I've told the story of each one. From childhood I'd looked at the braids, cornrows and extensions as a magical toolkit I could use to tell the world what my mark on it would be. And despite the roadblocks — feeling like I wasn't Black enough here, or too Black there — I am. I'm Black like me.

17 THE FRONT ROW

'It's "in" to use me and maybe some people do it when they don't really like me. But even if they are prejudiced, they have to be tactful if they want a good picture.'

NAOMI SIMS, *The New York Times*, 1969

'Black women are in fashion,' one editor casually said to me in Paris following a runway show.

The skin on my arms felt prickly and my stomach tight in the way it does when I feel a conversation taking a particular kind of turn. I found it curious that someone would use the temporal language ascribed to clothing and fleeting fashions to frame an entire people. It felt wrong. It sounded wrong. And yet I kept hearing similar observations while travelling the runway show circuit and doing all manner of panel discussions (so many panel discussions) about diversity and inclusion in fashion in general.

'With so many Black women appearing on magazine

covers and catwalks, do you think this is just another trend?' a White news anchor asked me another time, mid-broadcast.

Runway shows are a dime a dozen. There are shopping mall fashion shows. Church fashion shows. School charity fashion shows. And pet fashion shows. There are entire weeks filled with fashion shows in cities all over the world — among them Tel Aviv, Dakar, Dodoma, Lisbon, Bogotá, Liverpool, Reykjavik, Miami, Moscow, Copenhagen and Lagos. But only a few hold the kind of power that impacts the way people dress and perceive themselves. And they take place in just four cities: New York, London, Milan and Paris.

To sit in the front row of a luxury fashion show in one of these cities, home to the world's oldest and most storied houses, is to experience a unique set of conflicting emotions, particularly as a Black woman.

Because the rise of Black women is the talking point that has been most attached to the label of fleeting trend. One white editor went as far as to describe it to me as a bubble bound to burst.

On the surface, the front row is a thrill. There's the excitement of gaining entry to a rarefied world filled with the finest clothes human hands can make designed by some of the most skillful couturiers known to woman. A tiny little alternate universe populated by the affluent, influential, famous and the insiders powerful enough to determine who will become famous next. The front row is where the people deemed most integral to the success of those clothes — a mix of retailers, celebrities, stylists, journalists, popular Internet personalities and clients — converge. The spaces are limited. The invited are few. You know better than to consider inclusion a form of validation. The idea is intoxicating nonetheless. But below the surface, a seat on the front row for someone like me means a heightened consciousness of the many who are left out.

Navigating the front row can be an isolating and emotionally fraught experience for anyone. Its dramas have been well documented in all manner of books and films to varying degrees of accuracy — *Prêt-à-Porter, The Devil Wears Prada, Zoolander, The September Issue,* and more.

Will I get a seat? Where will I be seated? Who will I be seated next to? To many, these are all very important questions, without an ounce of irony. The answer can determine everything. How you're viewed by the rest of your peers. Your standing in a $2.4 trillion industry.

It's a century-old system built on art, desire, commerce, prestige, insider access and hierarchy. Power, buzz and influence come and go. One day you have it. Months, years or, if you're lucky, decades later, you don't. One minute you're in, the next you're out.

But lately, fashion has been rife with talk of the shift in who gets to be an insider and who gets to tell whose story. Because a dress is not just the covering on our backs, but a story of who we are, what we think, what tribe we belong to and how we view ourselves.

In the world of fashion, the reality of what is *in* fashion very much depends on who is in a position of power to declare it. Those who have an influential platform from which to tell the story determine the narrative. Anyone can claim red is the new black. But only a relatively small pool of people have the sway that can make it so. The problem is that the group dominating the storytelling, determining the trends on and off the runway, have been so homogenous, so overwhelmingly privileged and white. And, of the rest, even fewer are Black women. Of the designers working at a high level, there is Rihanna, Martine Rose, Grace Wales Bonner and Tracy Reese to name a small sampling from a fairly short list. Of the writers, editors and stylists in sufficiently senior-ranking positions at powerful enough publications to warrant a front row seat on the international circuit, just as few are Black women.

I came to fashion as an outsider. My earliest memories of the fashion show were not in Paris, Milan or London but in my grandparents' house, listening to my aunt recount her evening out attending the Ebony Fashion Fair, the travelling catwalk expo that operated from 1958 to 2009 and promoted the makeup line by the same name.

As a bank manager who lived and worked in Tidewater, Virginia, hers was a world away from the runways of Oscar de la Renta, Yves Saint Laurent and Valentino, and yet she knew who they were thanks to the fair which introduced luxury fashion to audiences of stylish Black women like my aunt nationwide. Ebony Fashion Fair came to fame in the Sixties, as Black Is Beautiful became a rallying slogan for growing Black pride. And like the Grandassa Models, a Harlem-based fashion show that celebrated natural Black beauty, each operated beyond the white gaze.

I never actually attended an Ebony Fashion Fair, a source of much personal regret. But as a child, I would study the images of Black and brown models, booted and dolman sleeved, in my grandparents' old issues of *Ebony* magazine, which once a year would turn into a promo for the fashion extravaganza. (Long before events became a much-needed revenue stream for magazines, Johnson Publishing Company had cracked that nut with *Ebony*.) I'd read the issues in my grandmother's house and feel like I was there, at Scope Exhibit Hall in Norfolk or Municipal Auditorium in Charleston, South Carolina, or Hixon Convention Center in Tampa, Florida. I could imagine the smell of perfume, hear the R&B soundtrack, and see the clothes sway and swagger.

My next encounter with the world of fashion was as a teenager attending a runway show at my local shopping mall sponsored by *Seventeen* magazine. I'd go with my mom and get styling advice about new ways to put together my Gap denim and Express sweaters for school. Meanwhile, pretty, photogenic, wide-eyed and wide-smiled local teens with names like Misty and Danielle would parade the runway hoping it would be a bridge to even bigger opportunities in Washington DC or even New York.

When I was a student at the University of Virginia, we'd have parties and a big annual fashion show during

Homecoming weekend, a time when the smaller Black student body would have our own lineup of events that ran parallel to the big keg-and-bowtie filled parties put on by the white fraternities and sororities. The fashion show was the highlight of the Black student body's social calendar and a kind of imitation of the legendary student fashion shows held at historically Black universities like Howard and Hampton. At UVA, it was less a catwalk show in the traditional sense, and more of a sexed-up theatrical production in which students wore the tightest or shortest or sheerest clothing possible (the guys would often go shirtless, their torsos oiled and bronzed to caricature levels). There would be dance interludes, involving body rolls, and slow dramatic walks to popular R&B songs like Ginuwine's 'Pony' — the models all at that stage of youth when the awkwardness of hormonal pubescence gives way to spectacular, unblemished beauty.

Students would have to audition by walking for a panel of judges made up of models who had walked in shows years before. Earning a spot in the cast was a badge of honour that secured social cachet and doubled one's dating prospects. During my freshman year (or 'first year' as all UVA students refer to it), only one girl from our entire class made the cut. I won a place in the show during my second year, along with four other classmates. We practised for months. And the night of the show, we fantasised that we were models in Paris, Naomi Campbell's long-lost cousins, twirling in couture.

It would be quite some time before I actually saw Naomi Campbell walk on a high fashion runway (Dolce & Gabbana, 2009) or attended my first couture show (Chanel, 2010). Back then, Black faces on the runway were fairly rare, and even more so on the front row.

But that has all changed in incremental steps. We have gone from the fringes to the forefront of the conversation, but we still aren't the primary storytellers and we remain criminally under-represented in positions of power behind the scenes.

Much has been made of the fact that we are at long last 'in'. Black women, but also a variety of women who exist beyond the narrow standard of old: Muslim women, non-binary women, women over the age of 50, little women, women with Down's syndrome, bigger women, wheelchair-bound women, and more.

But this language is inaccurate, because our emergence is not a fleeting trend in the manner of incoming skirt shapes and outgoing hemlines. Instead, it represents a paradigm shift away from fashion's entire history so far. Going back to its earliest days when Charles Frederick Worth created custom gowns for queens and princesses in the mid-nineteenth century, fashion has long existed around the famous, influential and aristocratic. And those groups were exclusively white until recently.

But fashion has spent the past decade slowly and finally opening its borders to communities of people who weren't included or even considered. If you ask these women, their inclusion is not a 'moment' but the result of tireless campaigns and organised efforts to break through mind-numbing homogeneity.

All it takes is a cursory glance at the landscape to get the gist. We've never had more visibility than we do now. This is particularly so with Black women, where our presence finally goes beyond the tokenistic one or two on the runways (Alek Wek, Liya Kebede, Adut Akech, Ajok Madel, Selena Forrest, Lineisy Montero, Imaan Hammam, the list goes on) and the covers of magazines (Beyoncé on *ELLE*, Rihanna on *Vogue*, Serena Williams on Harper's Bazaar, Lupita Nyong'o on everything).

As I write, the women who rank among the industry's most in-demand models include Adut Akech, a South Sudanese native born on the way to a refugee camp in Kenya, who now counts supermodel Naomi Campbell and Valentino creative director Pierpaolo Piccioli as her biggest champions, and Halima Aden, a Kenya-born, Missouri-raised hijabi who just five years ago was moonlighting as a cleaning woman, scrubbing toilets in St Cloud Hospital during her big debut runway season, in which she walked for Kanye West's Yeezy in New York and Max Mara in Milan. When the month of shows ended, Halima returned to her custodial job in Missouri until she reached a level of fame where she could afford to live on her model earnings.

There's also Paloma Elsesser, a London-born, Black American and Chilean-Swiss *Vogue* cover star who wears a size sixteen and actively campaigns for body positivity. And Indira Scott, a Jamaica Queens local best known for her waist-length, bead-embellished braids, a hair style she used to get bullied for wearing in school but is now a trademark that has gotten her runway jobs with Christian Dior. If one were to distil the shift in fashion down to a single visual symbol, Halima's hijab, Paloma's full, relatable figure or Indira's box braids would do. Each sparked conversation and headlines, yes, but each also run counter to the long, wispy Western ideal. Each also signifies a compelling story that has dominated not just the runways, but ad campaigns, magazine covers and social media impressions.

The beauty is in the breadth and the nuance of the representation — not seen since the Sixties and Seventies when the Grandassa Models and an overall rise in Black consciousness inspired a diverse movement in European fashion. The beauty is also in what this means for the waves of young girls who only know this moment of heightened visibility and nothing else, girls who will consider this the norm. Girls who will grow into women with a healthy sense of entitlement because of *course* they can be cover stars, and supermodels, and creative directors and CEOs.

It can be easy to boil it all down to trending, like a hashtag that gathers steam and then becomes yesterday's news. But this would be lazy. We are here, living, creating and flourishing, whether the fashion world chooses to tune in or not. Declaring a group of people 'in fashion' implies another group is out. And the suggestion that a group of people are out of fashion leads to the conclusion, no matter how knotty, of a scarcity complex and the feeling that there isn't room for all — not to mention the implication that we are present, not based on merit, but purely because we are trending.

This thinking undermines the power of the moment and the positive gains made by an industry that prides itself on progressive politics. It's the Alaïa-clad elephant in the room that reveals itself as and when the opportunity presents itself as it did a year ago when an editor casually remarked to me, 'We blondes are out of style right now', as we waited for a runway show in New York to begin. This thinking is the Achilles heel of the well-intentioned, exposing that the act of declaring a group of people in fashion, means one was likely complicit in that same group being out of it.

18 MODERN ACTIVISM

What good is a virtue signal really? Modern outrage tends to follow a series of steps that usually take place on the Internet. We read something. We get angry. We write a response. And post it. Maybe we'll sign a petition and post that. Or make a donation and post a prompt to do the same. Or post a call-out to meet somewhere and march.

We do something and then we move on, as does the news cycle. Modern outrage is transient.

But no matter what, its galvanising call-and-response usually takes place on social media.

One kind of modern activism, like the outrage that mobilises it, is grand, loud and performative — even when the action behind it is quite small. It's also the most popular kind, particularly in my network of passionate, outspoken opinion formers (some by trade, some by hobby), in the worlds of fashion and media. People who like to broadcast their actions and feelings.

The most long-lasting change, though, tends to come from the relentless, everyday activism, the kind that happens unnoticed in the day-to-day marathon of life — the small, sustained, daily acts of resistance that undermine forces of oppression and ultimately change shit. The kind that worked for countless generations before mine and those that follow.

The outrage usually comes fast and furious. It's unpredictable, popping up like tornadoes. What looks like a routine thunderstorm turns into something much worse, very quickly, decimating fields big and small. During a six-month stretch in 2019, the tornadoes of outrage that popped up in my feed, included but weren't limited to the following: a series of wildfires in the Amazon rainforest, Boris Johnson's suspension of Parliament, the seizure and separation of families at the American border, a six-year-old little girl arrested and jailed by Florida police for throwing a tantrum in class, the premiership of Boris Johnson, a series of Gucci turtleneck balaclavas that resembled Blackface, restrictive abortion laws in Alabama, an H&M campaign featuring a little Black girl with undone hair, a Twitter war between Donald Trump and John Legend and Chrissy Teigen, a young Black cisgender man's suicide after being bullied for dating a trans woman, mass shootings in El Paso Texas and Dayton Ohio, a Prada keychain that resembled the old racist character Sambo, the lack of press coverage of atrocities in Sudan, the lack of press coverage of atrocities in Kashmir... the list goes on and on.

And while the world events that sparked the outrage were unpredictable, the way in which it was expressed could not be more formulaic — through the extended Twitter thread, Instagram caption and Facebook status update.

Everyone is an activist, a changemaker. Influencers tag it onto the backs of their bios. But are they really? Are we?

In her rethinking of Black women's activism, Patricia Hill Collins describes how a 'Black mother who may be unable to articulate her political ideology but who on a daily basis contests school policies harmful to her children may be more an "activist" than the most highly educated Black feminist who, while she can manipulate feminist, nationalist, postmodern, and other ideologies, produces no tangible political changes in anyone's life but her own.'

Similar observations can be made today, when we have more language than ever before to articulate what we believe and what we don't — and are spoiled for choice about ways to voice it, a dizzying array of platforms in the palms of our hands.

What I've learned about activism is this: it must stay active. And the person I've learned this from is Bethann Hardison, a woman who over the course of many decades worked to get Black women greater visibility within the fashion world, a fight that to some might seem frivolous but in reality is one that ultimately impacts the way we see ourselves.

I developed my deepest sense of self at a time in my life when I felt most like a fly in a bowl of milk, my Blackness and Americanness solidifying in the most un-Black and un-American of settings: the fashion world in London in the early 2010s. James Baldwin once wrote that a lot of Americans moved away in order to get closer to themselves. This was certainly the case for me, the distance provided a mirror of sorts. But it was an opportunity I would not have had were it not for Bethann's strong encouragement as I agonised over two job offers: a senior editor role at a women's magazine housed in a large, cushy publishing company, or a global style director position abroad with a lesser-known title, with an even bigger reach, one that promised a working life traversing the global fashion circuit. 'Publishing jobs will always be here,' she told me. 'But an offer to move you across the world and see another kind of life, doesn't come so easily.' I took her advice and moved.

This was at a time when diversity and inclusion were not yet the thing – with a capital D&I – they would become and people still talked openly about adopting high-protein, low-carb diets in order to carve out thigh gaps large enough to make their legs look model-small in jeans. The terms body positivity and non-binary were largely unheard of. And young upstarts were more likely to refer to themselves as bloggers rather than influencers or activists as is their wont now.

When I attended my first big runway show in Paris, I counted two other identifiably Black faces in a room containing hundreds. One of them, a prominent older Black American journalist sitting front row, did not return my nod as we brushed shoulders on our way out of the crowded venue. I say this not to criticise the journalist, but rather to illustrate the time, one in which any sense of overarching community was replaced by competing, concentric circles of tightly knit colleagues. Brand was the shared experience that created alliance, rather than culture or ethnicity.

The business was largely filled with overwhelmingly white, mostly wealthy daughters of well-connected families or highly connected alumni of a small pool of influential fashion schools. People who could afford to be broke, their near non-existent entry-level income supplemented by flush parents for the first two to ten years it would take for them to earn a more liveable wage. Fashion was tribal, and I didn't necessarily fit into any one of the tribes.

I only knew one activist in the entire industry, Bethann, a godmother figure to virtually every Black person in fashion I know, including myself. And Bethann didn't even consider herself an activist. But she had been methodically advocating for and working towards a single goal for decades. She looked like an activist to me. And today she remains the woman many activists in the creative industries cite as an influence.

The steps in Bethann's activism looked quite different from the performative actions many take today.

Bethann came of working age in the Garment District during the Sixties, as the Black Panther Party, Southern Christian Leadership Council and Nation of Islam rose to national prominence. She later became a model, walking the runways of a new wave of icons in Paris including Issey Miyake, Claude Montana and Kenzo, as well as pioneering Black designers such as Willi Smith and Stephen Burrows. If the Grandassa Models amplified Black beauty to the Black community, Bethann and her peers, Pat Cleveland, Billie Blair, Alva Chinn and Amina Warsuma, became an unofficial coalition of women who broadcast Black beauty to the entire world. When they walked in the Battle of Versailles, a historic fashion event that pitted French designers such as Christian Dior and Hubert de Givenchy against American ones including Halston and Bill Blass — the models of colour numbering a ground-breaking ten — they introduced to the luxury fashion world a reality Black women had known all along: that Black is indeed very beautiful. This was 1973.

When she started her own model agency in the Eighties, she became known for her impeccable eye for new talent as she discovered and made the careers of a series of Black supermodels from Tyson Beckford to Veronica Webb. The founding publishing director of *ELLE* magazine, Regis Pagniez, credited Bethann with helping the new magazine earn a reputation for being more diverse and representative of modern life than its older competitors. In a *New York Times* article in 1986, *ELLE* is described as having 'refined the standard fashion magazine format', using 'many models of mixed ethnic heritage' and encouraging them to 'pose like they are in life'. *Paper* magazine exclusively used Bethann for their castings because her roster was more diverse than the other agencies. *Paper*'s editor in chief, Kim Hastreiter, praised Bethann for never ghettoising people but instead showing that 'beauty and fashion were (and still are) about all different colors. You represented girls of all ethnicities, including many white girls.' As other magazines scrambled to catch up, she founded the Black Girls Coalition to celebrate a new school of Black models who had come through including Karen Alexander, Cynthia Bailey and Naomi Campbell. This was 1988.

But when Bethann closed her business a decade later, moved to Mexico and took a break, the tide turned. A new wave of models washed in and swept Black models out of favour, kicking off a new era defined by a different look, one that problematically conflated the term 'aesthetic' with race. This was a time when hugely influential designers began showing their clothes on casts of exclusively white models — wispy, pale women from Eastern European countries rather than the diverse mix of women from Korea, Egypt, Nigeria, Angola, China and more who regularly star in it now. It was a samey blank canvas that permeated every nook and crevice of the fashion ecosphere. 'Designers wanted this ethereal girl that had no particular personality or look so that you only paid attention to the clothes. So they looked to Eastern Europe, which no one could really do before because the Wall was up. And it was a look that caught on like a brush fire. Other designers started to do it too and it kept going on and on and on until eventually the girl of colour was wiped out. I saw it happening, I saw how it happened,' Bethann explained to me. Few openly questioned the shift. This was 1997.

When I came along as a young, rising journalist ten years later and wrote my first piece about the paucity of non-white people on the runway and behind the scenes in the industry, few people, with the exception of Bethann, wanted to speak openly to me about their views. And when they did, they did so over the phone and over coffee in hushed tones, whispering the term 'racism'. To talk about race too much, too openly, was to be viewed as a gadfly, a troublemaker. This was 2007.

So Bethann called a small town hall meeting, inviting prominent editors, stylists, casting directors, model agents and other decision-makers in the industry to discuss the problem. And then she planned an even larger one, at the New York Public Library (which, full disclosure, I helped organise) followed by smaller talks and dinners. The industry responded slowly, the conversation inspiring spurts of progress including a special issue of *Vogue* Italy, dedicated to Black models.

Bethann kept the momentum going by forming a Diversity Coalition, an anonymous group of professionals of all races who she gathered to hold the industry accountable. They wrote open letters to the various governing fashion councils in New York, London, Milan and Paris. They named and shamed the fashion designers and labels who routinised the exclusion of non-white models. Suddenly, Black, brown and Asian models began appearing in larger numbers than the tokenistic one or two, with greater frequency. There were four at Céline, six at Calvin Klein and five at Prada. Gradually, the conversation became mainstream. Bethann no longer had to call out brands for exclusion. Consumers did, regularly and loudly.

And as I'd travel back to New York to cover the runway shows twice a year, I'd watch the cast of models and professionals filling the audiences become more inclusive in small increments. Bethann's daily, persistent activism over more than four decades changed the look of fashion, but she also helped change the culture of it as well. And while her work has commanded the attention of very famous people, brands and media platforms alike, the majority of the work was done quietly. 'When I addressed it, I never thought I couldn't change it. There's something in that,' Bethann told me one day over the phone as she prepared to head to Milan.

'If I thought someone wasn't doing the right thing, booking exclusively white girls, I would just speak to them about it. I noticed that *Brides* magazine never seemed to have brides of colour, not even a bridesmaid. I had to say to the editor, "You must think that Black people never get married." I'd say it just like that.'

In her address, 'Learning from the Sixties', Audre Lorde famously noted, 'revolution is not a one-time event. It is becoming always vigilant for the smallest opportunity to make a genuine change in established, outgrown responses.' Bethann understood the 'unromantic and tedious work necessary' to forge the 'meaningful coalitions' Audre spoke about. The steps in Bethann's activism were not complicated. They were repeated, ad nauseum, and refined with time. They did not dissipate when the news cycle moved on, as it inevitably does.

One need only scroll through the past year's worth of headlines in the fashion trades to understand that the business is still overwhelmingly white, and that brands and designers still regularly get inclusion wrong. Bethann remains, doing the work. But now, so does a loosely connected coalition of Black women, and men, across the world — editors, stylists, models and agents who would likely not be in their roles if Bethann hadn't kick-started a conversation about why more of us weren't. And like so many, I've tried to emulate Bethann in my own life, seeking out job candidates from outside the bubble of white privilege in British fashion one day, questioning an editor's observation that it would be odd to feature Black models in more than one fashion shoot in a single issue the next, picking up the phone to talk a young Black assistant through the frustration of being overlooked for a promotion another. Day after day, month after month, year after year.

'I concern myself about how it will matriculate into being what we want it to be. Will the change remain? Will it stay? You can have a conversation in 2007, but what's it going to look like in five years?' Bethann says. It's a conversation that has grown and evolved to include

Muslim people, Asian people, Latinx people, disabled trans people, poor people, the list goes on. This is 2020.

'I worry because I see how the same people who decide these trends are leaning so heavily into the West African girl. It's the way it's being done in which one girl looks so much like the other. My concern is balance, diversity. I want to see a Black girl, and a brown girl and an Asian girl, and a blonde girl. I always believed it would be okay. I just knew the work had to be there. Coming up against people, that ain't easy to do. It takes energy.'

I think about this most days as I swipe through an endless scroll of fury and outcry and wonder how we might use lessons from the activism of old to get the most impact out of the very powerful tools at our disposal, tools that the Sixties could only have dreamed of. How to take the best of both worlds — 'the power those who came before us have given us' as Audre said — to problem solve, which is essentially what activism is, in a better way.

I decided my form of activism would be the grass-roots approach of lifting as I climb. During dinner with a group of girlfriends one evening, women who were all an Only in their respective jobs in fashion and media like me, I decided to stop waiting for the big companies and governing bodies to fix the industry's homogeneity and use my platform to pull others in as I rose up the ranks. I contacted an old friend who is head of fashion at the Royal College of Arts and reached out to course leaders at Central Saint Martins and the London College of Fashion, telling them to send me their Black and brown students who showed talent and could benefit from mentoring. I in turn paired the students with my friends, women who had high-profile roles at top publishing houses, agencies and ready-to-wear brands. We helped them navigate school, internships, job interviews and entry-level positions. We showed them how to network properly and manage their finances. We bolstered their confidence. The mentees formed their own bonds with each other and became a support network separate from me and the mentors, using each other's talents to grow their own businesses and launch their own projects. Now, five years later, several of the mentees have become mentors. And many of them, including a West Indian designer from Lewisham and a Pakistani fashion writer from Croydon, are flourishing in high-profile roles of their own.

Beyond the satisfaction of playing midwife to a wave of new talent breaking through, the mentoring has helped me rekindle my own sense of optimism when the news cycle becomes overwhelming, which it always does.

19 ON QUEENIE

CANDICE CARTY-WILLIAMS

There's a lot to be said for the fact that when I started writing *Queenie*, I'd just turned 26. I wrote the majority of it in a small damp studio flat in Streatham. My housemates were mice and slugs, and the black mould that covered the walls was so thick that for the first time in my life, I had asthma. One very cold winter, my boiler broke and I had to get Environmental Health to call the landlord and force him to send a plumber out. When I started to write the book, I had no aspirations for it, or for myself. I wasn't thinking about money, and I wasn't thinking about Twitter followers. I only thought about who I was writing it for; the first audience was myself, and the second was all of the lonely Black girls and women who had been through some or all of the things Queenie would go through and had nobody to speak to about them.

I've definitely gone through some of the stuff Queenie has gone through. Mental health issues (I know them), bad dates (I absolutely know them) and identity issues rule much of my day. As I'll say more than once in this essay, and have said a million times in interviews, and will have as my epitaph, 'I am not Queenie'; but I knew I wasn't alone in some of the experiences I'd gone through, which in some form I needed to capture. I was also a lonely Black girl. I never felt like I fit into any group, into my family, into any actual unit. Talking about the book now, when I'm 30, has done very weird and wonderful things to my identity. I realised that every time I've been asked to talk about writing the book, I'd be taken back there. I was back to being that 26-year-old in that horrible flat, writing in bed to stay warm and doing probably irreparable damage to my back in the process. When I'd talk about the process of writing *Queenie*, I immediately forgot about anything I'd achieved since starting it.

A few months ago, I did one of many phone interviews. I like phone interviews because I can stay in my house. I'm not much of a people person. I don't think so anyway, but being an author has meant that I've sort of had to pretend to be one, but I'll come back to that. In this phone interview, I was caught off guard when the interviewer asked about the impact on my mental health that all the attention my book, and subsequently, I, had been getting. Now, I'm good at interviews; I've never had to worry about saying the wrong thing, or not being able to find the words. But this question stopped me in my tracks. It had been a long time since anyone, even friends and family really, had asked how I was. Not how the book tour was (long, lonely), how the book was selling (great, thanks), or, as a friend of mine once asked out of the blue, 'Have you been having loads of sex since you became famous?'

'I'm tired,' I said to the interviewer, surprising myself as I did. Was I truly that tired that the words jumped out? 'I'm overwhelmed. Every day. And I'm trying to be grateful and I'm trying to be in all of the places trying to inspire all of the people, but I'm struggling a lot.' It was the first time I'd said that, or even thought it. When I got off the phone, I started thinking about what I'd said. I started to interrogate how I'd been feeling. It's important to say that, generally, I interrogate all of my feelings. I don't mind how uncomfortable that makes me, because it's absolutely vital for me to get to the root of how I'm feeling. But this interrogation had to be a forced one.

What I realised was that I'd been wrapping my identity (of self, rather than character or characteristics — as Candice, a 29-year-old Black woman from south London) up in *Queenie* (the novel). This went deeper than me now not wanting people to think I was Queenie; this was about me linking how people were receiving the book with how they were receiving me as a person. All anyone ever wants to talk about is *Queenie*, when it's often the last thing I'm interested in discussing. I sort of couldn't believe that people couldn't separate me from my work, while they also couldn't separate me from the character I'd written. Funnily enough, before the book came out, I made sure that my hair didn't resemble the hair of the illustration on the book cover. Once, a friend came round and saw the advance copy of the book and asked, 'Is that your head??'

So, out came the twists and on went the headscarves. I refused to read from the book at events lest I invite the comparison, and in every single interview, even when I wasn't asked, I'd lead with 'This isn't autobiographical in ANY way... ' (Which still hasn't stopped people thinking I'm Queenie). Anyway, in my haste to separate myself from the fictional character, I hadn't thought about how I could bind myself, and my worth, up in the success of my work. Even though I'd previously thought I'd have that sort of self-preservation covered.

Writing this, I remembered a conversation I had with a DJ friend of mine I hadn't seen for a while. *Queenie* was just about to publish, and I was telling her about the journey I'd gone on to write the book, edit the book, find an agent, go to the meetings with editors, and get it published. As I was talking, she looked more and more concerned, which in turn made me concerned, and when I finished speaking, she said '... this is all great, but when you talk about it you're kind of talking about it as though it's someone else? You okay babes?' I think that was the point that I realised I'd subconsciously created a whole new identity. I think I'd created an identity beyond myself: that of an author. I wasn't willing to let my life go. I didn't want to be someone who just spoke about my work.

That identity, the one that almost had *me* speaking about Candice the author in the third person, was just one identity I've created, and have upgraded in the last couple of years. That identity, but the upgraded 2.0 version, is People-Facing Candice. People-Facing Candice loves talking to readers who want to talk to her about the things they've been through, or the ones who want to ask questions about what's next for Queenie. People-Facing Candice loves talking to the press, especially when they ask invasive questions about her personal relationship to sex, and People-Facing Candice doesn't mind when people come up to her when she's looking and/or feeling her very worst on the tube and ask for a selfie.

When I started with this author business, I genuinely thought that my job, as someone who wrote books, was going to be to… write. Even though I worked in book publishing for years, somehow I forgot that writers have to publicise the book. We actually have to get out of our pyjamas and emerge from our hovels blinking into the light, and stand in front of people and talk about the book. I know that I have never, and will never, like public speaking, and I still struggle with the reality of it being something that's about to happen days before an event. Before one talk I was doing at 7.30 p.m., all I could manage for the whole day was a biscuit. One biscuit. That's the funny thing about writing; you spend your whole day (or night, in my case) being solitary, silent, for months, maybe years on end. You get comfortable with being alone. You get comfortable telling people that they won't see you for a while because you're working. And then, one day, after all of those solitary days, you're thrust in front of an audience, squinting when the bright lights hit the eyes that have been focusing on your laptop screen in the dark, and you have to perform. We didn't plan for this! We didn't rehearse for this! The disconnect between doing the work, and being the work, is a hard one to navigate.

On not being a people person: I used to be someone who thought of herself as an introvert. Being a self-confessed introvert was a very comfortable and safe part of my identity. It meant that when I was out, I could get away with only talking to my friends and not engaging with anyone new. None of my friends thought I was rude, they just put it down to my introverted nature. It also meant that I could quite happily say to colleagues, 'Why would I come to the pub after work when I've seen you all week?' and they'd all say, 'Fair enough, that's just Candice', rather than be offended. I cannot get away with this any more. I have to be *on* when I'm being an author. All of that wanting to hide behind introversion has got to go out the window.

While I am supremely grateful for everything that's happened to me, I'm still scared of it, I don't know if I'll ever get used to it. But maybe that's a good thing. As we get older and we change and we find different paths and new circles, and answer new callings, our identities are in various states of flux anyway. All of the identities that I hold, and project, come from me, and are all legitimate versions of me. I just need to learn how to be comfortable in that, and to remind myself that each identity is just as valid as the other. You know what, though? The more time I spend as People-Facing Candice, the more that identity dominates the rest of them. I kind of... like talking to loads of people now, even when it makes me uncomfortable. I don't mind putting that discomfort aside if it means someone can come away from talking to me and say that I made them feel better, or that I answered a burning question they had about why Queenie doesn't date Black men.

Actual Candice, me, is a very sensitive person. It's almost unbelievable how soft I am. I'm very quiet, observant, very still, and prefer to listen than to speak. I usually have my hood up to block out the world, and my glasses off so that everything I look at is softer around the edges, less sharp, less in focus. I would rather die than actively upset someone, and in conversations do actual mental acrobatics to make sure I'm making people as comfortable as possible. Take this sensitive Candice, throw her in the spotlight, and what else could I do but create a whole new persona to deal with being actively recognised and spoken to?

All this identity work goes back to how I see myself; I finally see myself as an author, which took long enough. For a long time, I'd look confused when I was introduced as one. I finally see myself as someone who has valid opinions, and I am finding my confidence when it comes to expressing them. I can also now see that identities don't have to be one or the other. Identities don't have to be binary. The whole introvert versus extrovert label that I'd been so obsessed with adhering to stopped being as clear-cut to me. Then, someone told me, not long after meeting me, that they didn't think I was an introvert at all. They said I struck them as more of an anti-social extrovert. I liked that. It helped me to see that as much as we can prescribe to, or hide behind, the social markers of what identity is, it doesn't really mean anything at all. Because someone will always take you for the version of you that they want, whatever you're trying to project, or whoever you're trying to be. The idea of identity is hard enough when we're trying to work out who we are in this world. Add to that the effort of trying to manage the identity you project to people and you're done for. No wonder I was so tired.

20 BAD BITCHES

The Internet has several definitions for Bad Bitch. According to Urban Dictionary, she is:

Totally mentally gifted and usually fine as hell.

An amusing, inspiring, fun-loving and independent bosslady who is mentally gifted and also fine as hell.

A female who knows what she wants and knows exactly how to get it. A female who is always ready for anything physically, emotionally, and also intellectually (one being book smart as well as street smart). One who is classy and all about business. Last but certainly not least one who knows how to take care of her man at home and in the streets and remains loyal to him, herself and the game at which she plays.

That is just one of many entries, but the gist is clear. A bad bitch is a lot of things. Probably too many things for one woman to live up to. But she is usually Black — the phrase was popularised in hip-hop and remains a mainstay in rap lyrics from Lil' Kim and Jay-Z to Lizzo and Cardi B — and always a woman.

I love Black women. I love us with a pure, bottomless,

concentrated, no-added-ingredients kind of adoration that goes beyond the love I have for my mother, sister, aunts or even myself.

Rather, it's an enduring devotion rooted deeply in our stories; the winding, bendy, journeys through small setbacks and enormous obstacles that make each of us who we are. The full lives that make each of us bad. Not bad meaning bad, but bad in the Run DMC sense. Bad meaning good. Better than good. Excellent. Goals. Magic. Bad bitches.

I love us. We are beautiful, powerful, queens. Master of slays. Leader of movements. Makers of culture and changer of games. We are Michelle Obama's leadership. Grace Jones' radicalness. Maxine Waters' candour. And Tarana Burke's compassion. Yara Shahidi's optimism. Dina Asher-Smith's speed. Serena Williams' stamina. And Sade's elegance. Ava DuVernay's vision. Patrisse Cullors' activism. Missy Elliott's innovation. And Megan Thee Stallion's knees. We are all these things and more.

But in the course of writing this book, and contemplating my own experiences, it's dawned on me that as we celebrate our heightened visibility in this era of inclusivity, the spotlight moves ever more in the direction of the exceptional, leaving many out.

I have grown tired of conversations that only look at our exceptionalism in relation to misconceptions about us. And I have also grown equally tired of conversations where we must explain our chosen states of being, whether that be self-improving, excelling and flexing or slowing down, muddling through and figuring it all out.

White people aren't expected to slay all day. And when they do, they aren't asked to defend said excellence. Why should we?

Yes, we slay. But Black Girl Magic is not just in the headline-making feats but in the magic of just being. Unbothered. Unencumbered. No questions answered, except those asked of ourselves.

It's about the right to be a superwoman one day. Regular degular the next. Messy another.

Graduate degrees popping... or not. Hair and nails did... or not. Skin a little broken out... or not. Dream job offers forever out of reach... or not. Twerk a little off-rhythm... or not. Love life in the toilet... or not. Family dynamic a struggle... or not. Finances on fleek... or the opposite. House and wardrobe Instagrammable... or not.

The right to inhabit it all. It's a luxury that seems to elude most of us. But rather than wait for it to be granted, maybe it's time to create it for ourselves.

'Sometimes, I wish I was not a bad bitch all the time,' an attractive woman in a support group on the HBO comedy series, *A Black Lady Sketch Show*, asks, her lace front thick and shiny, her makeup a full beat to Pat McGrath levels of perfection.

The other bad bitches in the group recoil in loud, audible horror, long gel nails clutching virtual pearls.

'I want to wear normal house slippers. Not three-inch-heel house shoes,' another adds.

'Stop whining. Being a bad bitch is an honour. We didn't choose this life. This life chose us,' a third woman,

Afro and smoky eyes full and flawless, says, indignant with outrage.

The other women, including Laverne Cox, lips lacquered in red, arms stacked with bangles, agree.

'There is nothing wrong with being an okay bitch as long as you not a basic bitch,' the group leader, Queen Bad Bitch Angela Bassett, cheekbones contoured and shoulders clad in fur, declares, settling the score.

As the women offload, the camera pans to a secret observation room and the viewers realise what the bad bitches don't. They're not in a support group, but a controlled medical study for Fashion Nova, the top-selling women's apparel brand known for churning out bodycon dresses for the likes of Cardi B, Kim Kardashian and Nicki Minaj. Each bad bitch has been medicated to acclimate to the undue pressures of bad bitchdom.

The vignette in writer, actress and comedian Robin Thede's hilarious series is a switchblade-sharp commentary on impossible beauty standards. But its punchline is also transferrable to any one of the many irritating expectations that can thwart us.

As women, we're often the recipients of instruction that was not asked for and policing that is not required. This is even more so for Black women, who have been subjected to a long history of systemic policing – of our bodies, behaviours and our beings. Profitable careers have been built doing exactly this.

To tell a woman how to live is big business. The self-help industry generates revenue that rivals professional sports. The phenomenon of the bad bitch was commercial enough to land Amber Rose a book deal writing a manual that would teach women how to become exactly that. In a statement, Rose defined 'bad bitch' as a 'self-respecting, strong female who has everything together. This consists of body, mind, finances and swagger; a woman who gets hers by any means necessary.'

To be sold unsolicited advice and be gifted with unasked for expectation, is not just a Black woman thing. It's a woman thing. But I can only speak to the particularity of my experience, which is not only inextricably tied to gender, but race, education and class.

The idea of the bad bitch is not new.

For many of us, the notion that we had to be firing on all cylinders, at all times, was baked into our upbringing, with parents in all corners of the diaspora going so far as to instil in their children the idea of having to be twice as good as their white peers in order to earn just as much. A self-fulfilling maxim born out of the Jim Crow era and civil rights movement that followed, it permeated not just the parenting style of generations, but our entertainment, social groups and literature. It also birthed the bad bitch.

I can't remember when or where I first heard the mantra; I don't recall my parents ever uttering the words 'twice as good' or 'just as much'. But I remember the sentiment being all around me — at family gatherings, in Sunday Bible school, during play dates with friends, and in the episodes of *The Cosby Show* I watched as a kid — colouring my childhood with a particularly bright shade of strive.

Any child or grandchild of the civil rights generation understood the lesson: due to an uneven playing field, it would require exceptional effort in order to achieve what the average white person might view as ordinary. And the effort was mandatory. The feeling among my elders always seemed to amount to the message that our ancestors didn't come this far for folks to lighten the grip on their bootstraps — even as time and world events made it increasingly plain to all of us that respectability doesn't really matter. That no post-graduate degree, high-powered job or rock-solid credit score can protect you from the indignity of being followed by a security guard in a shop or mistaken for being the nanny of your light-skinned baby in the park.

The 'twice as good' idea also played out for many of us on a generational front, the idea that we needed to accomplish twice as much as our forbears to keep the momentum of progress going. My parents, grandparents, aunt and uncles didn't have to spell out to my sister and I that we were expected to grow up and surpass the generations that had come before us in terms of achievement. It was obvious. And for whatever reason, I never questioned it. Maybe I never questioned it because this thinking was all I knew. The idea of excellence was tied to purpose, community growth and uplift.

This feeling carried over into my university life, where I was surrounded by a small but robust network of students who lived Black excellence on various levels. I acquired girlfriends in bulk — a high-achieving mix of

former valedictorians and class presidents, all unapologetically outspoken, all stylish, all swaggerific and beautiful.
It was invigorating, if a little sickening. These were bad
bitches in training. They watched *Daughters of the Dust*
and could offer a critical analysis of the repertoire of
Tupac and Notorious B.I.G. They looked camera-ready
without makeup and had regular hair appointments,
while I mostly did my own clumsy wash and wraps in my
dorm room and struggled to find the right MAC concealer
to match my skin tone. I was awkward in comparison
and much more of a work in progress than they looked
to my eyes. Nevertheless, I found their friendship exciting
and energising.

We formed a network that became a safe space as
we went on to push into largely white work settings
post-college, as young attorneys, medical trainees, writers,
editors, doctors and investment bankers, traversing all the
pressures these environments come with, as well as the
expectations of our families, and ourselves.

But the tone and tenor of the expectations I encountered changed as I progressed in the world of media,
and found myself swinging up the rungs in tandem with
the rising Internet boom, which provided exponentially
more space for critique and discussion about everything.
Alongside this, a new wave of feminism emerged in the
2010s together with the first-person essay economy, and
the two combined to create an environment rife with
opinionators, deep dives and hot takes, all travelling at
the speed of 4G and intensifying our ambitions.

And throughout, Black women were magic and slayed all day. On the tennis court. On the stage. On the big screen. And at the polls. And moves that would not make headlines had the executor been white (being elected to office in certain cities, for example) became the subjects of rounds of analysis and discourse.

Bad bitches were everywhere. As The Only. The First. The All Too Sporadic Moment in some incredibly long time. We revelled in being #carefreeBlackgirls. And living our best #Blackgirljoy. We got in formation and documented the glory of our visibility in beautifully arranged tableau, clothes coordinated in tonal variations, faces bright with accomplishment. All united under the wonder of #Blackgirlmagic. Our ancestors' wildest dreams.

But gradually, the idea that we are magic and the notion of slaying became talking points that only applied to women of a certain type: marketable, camera-ready, and relatively affluent with quotable sound bites at the ready, sexy backstories and a large following tuned in to their every move.

And the magic in the ordinary began to get left out, lost.

Around this time, I was overachieving with the best of them. Off the back of my graduate studies at Oxford University, which I had completed during the two-year stretch when I was pregnant and on mat leave, I joined the editorial staff at *ELLE*, eventually climbing the ranks to become deputy editor, the most senior role ever held by a Black woman at the British luxury fashion magazine.

While there, I established a mentoring programme to help fix the criminal scarcity of people of colour working behind the scenes in the country's £26 billion clothing industry. While doing all of this, I juggled television appearances, talks, columns and television and radio broadcasts. I said yes to the opportunities that intrigued me. No to the projects that didn't. And throughout everything, I was a mother and a wife. Here is where I should add that, with the exception of my mentoring, this mix of work is not particular to race but instead the very unique experience of working in media in the 2010s.

Nonetheless my work was often ascribed to race.

'Black girl magic goals!' captions would sometimes read underneath my Instagrams, broadcasting my latest article, project or musing. I'd post a waving Black girl emoji in response to the rallying cry.

'I don't know how you do it. Aren't you tired?' colleagues and peers on the fashion circuit would ask.

The question would routinely annoy me. These were all things I liked, no loved, doing. A happy wife makes a happy life and all that. A fulfilled mom means happy kids, etc, etc.

But if I dug a little deeper I would have arrived at a more honest answer to that question, which would have been yes. I was tired, yes. But mainly tired of the explaining. I was fine minding my own business doing things I enjoyed, working to create opportunities for myself so that I could in turn provide opportunities for younger people like me and eventually my kids. But I was also tired of feeling the weight of responsibility to help fill a crucial gap in an entire industry. Tackling microaggressions on the job, while supporting other Black women who were The Firsts and The Onlys to do the same. I was willing and ready to do the work, I just wished there weren't so much of it to do.

What underlines all of this is privilege. The privilege of being able to afford the childcare that allows me to do a job I love that has raised my profile enough to be able to do projects, like this book, that I find personally fulfilling.

But increasingly I've discovered the real personal growth happens in the ordinary day-to-day moments rather than the big, life-defining ones. The unnewsworthy and unremarkable, but no less meaningful. It's in the one-to-one exchanges with my closest girlfriends about the banalities that don't make the highlights reels — the pushing through and the figuring it all out, the winning and the fucking it all up. To me, this is where the magic is.

The origins and the ownership of the phrase 'Black Girl Magic' has been subject to much debate in recent years. But most agree writer Joan Morgan was one of, if not the definitive, first to put it out into the world through her 2000 book, *When Chickenheads Come Home to Roost*, a cleverly titled collection of writing that excellently captured, chronicled and interrogated the rise of hip-hop feminism. Interestingly, she writes of a Black girl's magic in an essay about her rejecting the unrealistic notion of the Strong Black Woman, the original Bad Bitch.

In a passage describing how she left New York to seek a slower pace in California, she wrote:

In Frisco I did a few wonderful things. I fell apart regularly in the arms of two deliciously brown men (one a lover, both friends) who faithfully administered the regular doses of TLC I needed to breath again — unafraid of my tears or fragility. I wrote. Spent lots of time near the water. Heard Oshun's laughter twinkling like bells, urging me to recapture the feminine and discovered the fierceness of a Black girl's magic. I did and had what I now know to be a powerfully feminist time. Back then though, I was just saving my life.

Thirteen years later, CaShawn Thompson, a mother, wife and Early Care and Education Specialist, based in the Washington, DC area began using the hashtag #Blackgirlsaremagic as a source of uplift. 'The hashtag was born of a childhood understanding of how wonderful Black women are. I first used it in a Tweet in response to someone saying that Serena Williams looked like a man and that is why she was a superior athlete,' she told me. In an interview with the writer Feminista Jones she explained, 'The difference was, I was the first person to use it and reference Black girl empowerment. Other times it was used before, it was always something about Black girls' and Black women's hair. I was the first person to use Black Girl Magic or Black Girls Are Magic in the realm of uplifting Black women. Not so much about our aesthetic but just who we are.'

The phrase spread in her network and a friend suggested she put it on a T-shirt. She sold 330 within weeks.

The hashtag, which Black Twitter eventually abbreviated to #Blackgirlmagic, grew from there, becoming a global phenomenon that transcended borders, rousing generations of women around the world. It spoke to me, and the women I knew, as well as an entire world of people — of all races and backgrounds — who I didn't. The hashtag became a cultural moment in itself, even as it celebrated a series of cultural moments. And in the process the phrase became associated with the superlative: the record-breakers and the history-makers.

Simone Biles wins five Olympic gold medals #Blackgirlmagic

Dina Asher-Smith becomes the fastest woman in the world #Blackgirlmagic

Beychella #Blackgirlmagic

Rihanna becomes the first Black woman to launch a fashion label funded by LVMH #Blackgirlmagic

Google dedicates an ad to Black Girl Magic #Blackgirlmagic

It speaks volumes about the trajectory of Black Girl Magic that the Google ad about #Blackgirlmagic failed to include the woman who popularised the phrase, a move that devastated Thompson.

'Because women like me have always been erased or taken out of stories, one way or the other,' she told *The Root*. 'Women like me — poor women, poor Black women; women that — like I do — work at day cares, women that work at CVS; women that wear their hair a certain way, women that talk a certain way; women that didn't go to college, or didn't finish. You know, those of us that exist on the margins, even within Black communities; those of us that aren't traditionally looked at as "Black excellence".'

Thompson wasn't the only one who felt left out.

My friend Amy is a woman who on paper has all the qualities of a bad bitch (law degree, gorgeous Brooklyn loft, Morehouse alum husband and a Gap ad gorgeous son). Those gleaming, inspiring women I described from uni? She was one of them and to this day is at the centre of the group of women who make up my safe space. Amy, a woman who our mutual friends routinely refer to using the word 'goals', admits to feeling displaced by it. 'I feel like I'm surrounded by all these unicorns with these colourful manes, everyone killing it. But I feel like this idea of Black Girl Magic doesn't always leave room for the ones who are just trying to figure it all out and that's because we don't always get to see the fallible as powerful.'

Issa Rae voiced similar concerns when doing the press rounds for her show *Insecure*. 'We don't get to just be boring,' she said about her show, which stands out in the television landscape for depicting Black women as being ordinary. The great irony: critics hailed the simple act as revolutionary.

To be clear, this is not an anti-Black Girl Magic treatise. Instead, it's commentary on the celebrification of it and a case for steering the movement back to where it originated, a place that highlighted the magic in the regular degular, whether that be figuring out a way to get your child collected from summer camp at a moment's notice when your husband drops the ball or managing to roll out of bed, step into the shower, and resume a job search when a string of demoralising phone calls from a debt collector has you wanting to do otherwise. A space where the okay bitch is a bad bitch and the bad bitch can just be. Free.

EPILOGUE

THE WAY WE GRIEVE

Words are no match for death. When Eric Garner gasped, 'I can't breathe', as New York City Police officers choked him to death on a busy Staten Island street on a summer's day in 2017, his cry fell on deaf ears — as did the very same words when George Floyd uttered them in May 2020, three years later, as a police officer choked all the life out of him in front of a food shop in Minneapolis.

And yet words help keep the dead alive, enshrining the memory of a life in history. This ritual, the practice of memorial, has historically been left to the eulogy and the obituary, pieces of writing normally authored by family members and friends — a highlights reel of one's milestones, achievements, and deeply personal, pivotal moments. But what happens when the Internet and social media do the eulogising? What happens when the tributes stop being about the dead, but instead about the people processing the news of the dead?

One day you're alive, living, breathing and full of promise as 19-year-old Oluwatoyin 'Toyin' Salau was.

The next day, you're not. Life cut short and memorialised in grid form. One day, you're known among your immediate family and friends. The next day, you're a hashtag, a headline and a Wikipedia page, a Google trail that has sprung up overnight as word of your death spreads on social media, and digital press outlets race to rank first on your name.

This is uniquely different from the way the world grieves the death of a celebrity, though to die the way George or Toyin did means that one becomes extremely well known. Your face becomes ingrained in the memory of the public. It's painted, illustrated and surrounded by flowers with artful type running underneath it. You become a digital asset — eye-catching and square shaped so that it can be easily shared, screen-grabbed and re-shared, giving people an easy visual to accompany their own reflections about you or themselves. Prominent politicians, activists and celebrities speak out in your memory and raise legal and funeral funds for your family. You become the latest face of a movement. But you're not here. Not living. Not breathing. All that promise, cut short.

I started writing this epilogue about the unjust killing of George Floyd and how it devastated so many Black mothers like me, hearing him cry out for his own mother while a police officer suffocated him. I started writing about how this experience is heartbreakingly shared by many Black women, praying for the safety of our sons, brothers and fathers in the face of a world that routinely brutalises Black men. I thought about my own experiences as I sifted through a wave of grief and testimonials on social media. George Floyd's death had not only sparked a wave of outrage and activism against police brutality, but a global movement in which we began to interrogate every aspect of racism.

Then news of Breonna Taylor's unjust killing broke and we all learned of how three police officers gunned her down, shooting her eight times in the night during a no-knock raid on the wrong home. We saw images of her with her girlfriends and family members, smiling and carefree. We read her Tweets. She was optimistic about her future. She was ambitious. She could have been any of us. So we eulogised her, by talking about how her death impacted us and how as Black women we have to advocate for ourselves and each other, always. Because if we don't, there will be no national outcries for justice. We talked about our trauma, our grief. And I began to instead make this epilogue about the experience of being a Black woman thrust into the role of educator, one repeatedly asked to comment on Black pain and explain how racism works to a wider, White audience while processing grief. (Something, mind you, I refused to do.)

We then learned of Tony McDade, a transgender man killed by a police officer responding to a call about a stabbing. And then Toyin was found dead a week after Tweeting that she had been sexually assaulted. Toyin Oluwatoyin, Yoruba for 'God is worthy of praise.' We lifted her up. We said her name. In the process, we shared our own experiences of neglect and abuse.

The hashtags were coming too fast and furious. The more lives lost, the more words were written. White people, newly awakening to the reality of racism, confessed past misdeeds and owned up to their privilege, while Black people gave testament to the reality we knew all along: racism has always been here. We were grieving the loss of another life. But this time, Black people weren't the only ones doing it. For the first time, people from all walks of life, the world over, were speaking out in solidarity with Black Lives Matter. We grieved the brutal killings of women and men we didn't know. We saw ourselves in them. Their deaths had compelled us to look inward.

The experience of considering one's own life experience in the face of death is not new. We try to find meaning in the latter, and make sense of the former. In her memoir, *Death of Innocence: The Story of the Hate Crime That Changed America,* Emmett Till's mother, Mamie Till-Mobley, wrote, 'When I am out and about, people recognise me and they want to talk about him, what his death meant to them, what I mean to them still. They just can't help it.'

Only now, we broadcast it to each other. During the weeks following George's murder, everyone had said all the things on social media, television, radio and in print, but words and performative outrage wouldn't bring back 26-year-old Breonna or 25-year-old Ahmaud, or give George breath, or promise my son a future in which Black Lives Mattering was not a debate and police brutality against Black people not a public health crisis.

My closest girlfriends and I had been agonising over how to discuss Black Lives Matter with our small boys. Because, of course it matters. It's been mattering. I mean think about it, it's hard to learn that people don't like you because of the colour of your skin,' one of them explained. My son had not seen the footage that sparked the fires burning in America; a white police officer, Derek Chauvin, pinning George face down to the ground, using his knee to kneel his entire body weight onto the unarmed man's air passageway for 8 minutes and 46 seconds. My son didn't have to.

Talk of George surrounded us, even in COVID quarantine. As much as my husband and I tried to ration our news intake around the kids, the story was there. On CNN, as we channel surfed our way to the children's networks. On BBC Radio 4 and WNYC as we cooked. During our social distanced strolls through the park with friends. In the Black Lives Matter signs that began hanging in windows in our neighbourhood.

'What if we go back to America and what happened to George happens to me?' my son asked me one morning as we listened to a radio broadcast about the riots that had erupted in America. I didn't know what to say. I told him he is loved, valued, intelligent, a child of God and the firstborn son of Matt and Kenya, a gift we prayed for. I told him he stands on the shoulders of all who have come before him, a people who have survived World Wars, Jim Crow, enslavement, the Middle Passage. I joked and told him he's a Hunt and a McGuinness, the product of strong stock. I said a lot of things. But I wasn't sure if any of those things answered his question. So I hugged him. Held him close and quietly observed the stillness in his face, the sadness and confusion that seemed to be settling in as he tried to process it all. In parenting him, my husband and I have always made it a priority to ensure he associates Blackness with love, joy and prosperity rather than oppression and suffering. This is a child whose first President was a Black man. It was a great source of pride for me that a Black President was the only President my son knew for the first years of his life. Not that this could protect him from the realities of racism.

I can't breathe. The tragedy of these words becoming a hashtag against the backdrop of a COVID-19 pandemic, a virus that ravages the lungs, and has hit the Black population hardest of all, was too much for the heart to take. But I can't breathe also became the thing that re-sensitised us to humanity and mortality after months and months in which coronavirus death tolls had become so high that we practically stopped noticing, the numbers in the headlines looking like distant, abstract figures. I can't breathe. The words took on a life beyond the man and became a call to action for us all, appearing on T-shirts, in murals and on protest placards.

I can't breathe. I had no words. Grief filled my mind like a fog. Grief for Breonna and Toyin. And so many others from Sandra Bland to Eric Garner and back to Emmett Till and beyond. Grief that their deaths had touched my son and his own understanding of how people regard one another.

George Floyd and the police brutality that cut his life short was not only the talk of America, but the UK. The world. As the outrage turned into protests, riots and a global social justice movement, the fury became less about George Floyd and more about us.

And the thing powering our connectivity — those, blue-lit square boxes — began to feel less like a conduit to a warm comforting bond and more like a compulsion. We needed a break from our scrolls, because between COVID, escalating racial conflict and the unexpected passing of heroes from John Lewis to Chadwick Boseman, our feeds had begun to feel like an endless obituary. Yet there was the overwhelming sense that we couldn't afford not to tune in. The defining losses and gains were coming so thick and fast. Social media was the platform for both our comfort and horror; the tool we used to organise, but also the very thing that threatened to mentally and emotionally undo us.

Nevertheless, Black women mobilised and served as beacons and stabilisers throughout it all. There was Kamala Harris making history as both the first Black American and Asian American woman to run for Vice President on a major party ticket. The non-binary activist Janaya Khan delivering live Sunday Sermons speaking to a range of pressing issues including 'the ways in which we casually throw aside Black women, Trans women of colour and all the in-betweens'; BLM founder Patrisse

Kullors leading live Daily Digests, in which she'd give a debrief about the latest developments in the social justice movement and talk viewers through how to keep showing up and convert heartbreak, outrage and fatigue into action; and on a lighter but no less impactful note, TikTok star Tabita Brown talking to her nearly 4.5 million-strong following through trauma with mellifluous-voiced humour, wisdom and vegan food.

Black women had become the face of a historic year, once again blanketing September issue magazine covers, their faces next to cover lines that read like protest slogans ('The Time Is Now' on *T Magazine*), their portraits taken by fellow Black women (Amy Sherald's touching painting of Breonna Taylor for *Vanity Fair*) and in the cases of American and British *Vogue*, serving as the look of hope.

We continued to show up.

'How are you doing in the midst of all of this?' I WhatsApped one of my closest friends shortly after footage of a police officer shooting an unarmed Jacob Blake in front of his three children was released. 'Girl' she replied. The word spoke multitudes. She didn't need to say more, but she did. 'I'm still here. I'm still rising.'

THANK YOUS

I could not have written this book without Matthew McGuinness, the great love of my life and father of my two boys. Thank you for giving me the time and space to do this, for being a constant sounding board and creative partner, for listening to me workshop my essays in the ungodly hours of the night when you wanted to just roll over and fall asleep, but always stayed up to read and feedback first. Thank you to my mother and father, for giving me the boundless love, support, friendship and courage to go out into the world and take risks by constantly reminding me that I can always come home. Thank you for the example of your life and love, and for always inspiring me to do better. In a way this book starts with my parents, because they were the beginning of me.

To my sister, April, and to my girlfriends, Amy and Kathleen, I see you. I love you. I am forever grateful for you and the safe space that we have between us. My girls! Thank you for inspiring me, and for answering my many, many, many calls, texts and WhatsApps throughout this whole writing journey.

Thank you to Candice Carty-Williams, Ebele Okobi, Freddie Harrel, Jessica Horn and Funmi Fetto for contributing your powerful stories. Reading your words reminded me all over again (not that I ever needed reminding) why I love Black women.

Big gratitude to my agent Kate, who helped me take *GIRL* from a germ of an idea during a catch-up call to completion and has championed the book, with heart-warming enthusiasm, from day one, shepherding it through these COVID-times.

Thank you to everyone at the HQ family: Charlotte Mursell for your early belief in the book, Rachel Kenny for being such a dedicated, supportive and thorough editor. A special thank you to Lisa Milton for the opportunity and to Melissa Kelly, Lily Capewell, Nira Begum, Kate Fox and everyone at HarperCollins UK who helped bring *GIRL* into the world.

A special thank you to the women in my family who had such an indelible impact on me: my grandmother Bessie, my late aunt Verna, my aunt Gloria, cousin Ruth, late aunt Gail and cousin Camille. Thank you to my former Professor Deborah McDowell for allowing me to see first-hand what I knew I wanted to be: an author.

I'm eternally grateful for my dear friends — Michelle, Tola, Nana, Melinda, Rosa, Roger, Malcolm, Lauren, Sherry, Luella, Ije, Chiemeka, Mitzi and Tina — and all the years of love.

And last, but not least: my beloved, effervescent sons, Cosmo and Bruno. Thank you for your patience with me as I wrote this. Long weekends of Lego and Minecraft await.